WIN the FIELDS

Articles written by Lou Burruss

Published by Skyd Magazine

Win the Fields

ISBN: 9780996310727

Skyd Press
Seattle, WA

Cover image by Sandro Schuh

Design by Adam Restad
AR Design

Win the Fields

CONTENTS

Articles edited with great care by Jonathan Neeley.

In 1990, Lou was born into ultimate behind the library on the Carleton College campus winning his first game ever, a 11-10 3rd Goodhue v. 2nd Goodhue grudge match. He played for the B Team his freshman year and then four years for CUT, reaching the semis at Nationals twice. Moving to Seattle, Lou played ten years for the Fish, winning a World's gold (97), bronze (02) a Nationals gold (04) and three silvers (96, 97, 05). As a coach, Lou led Syzygy for four years (97-00) winning gold (00) and two silvers (98, 99). Since moving to Oregon, he has coached Fugue 4 years and won a title in 2010.

Lou Burress has been a contributor for Skyd Magainze since 2011 and has published over 30 articles over the past four years in his column *Win the Fields*.

INTRODUCTION

By Elliot Trotter

Lou Burruss is a busy guy. Between coaching the University of Oregon's Fugue to multiple college championships and finals appearances, commentating at world championships events, Lou is a family man and possesses a uniquely curious mind. It seems that Lou is always reading a new book or trying to further his understanding of coaching philosophy or player psychology. I wouldn't put an atlas of human anatomy past Lou's reading collection, as he's the type of guy who is constantly trying to better his understanding in whatever way possible.

It took about three months to wrangle Lou from his personal blog to Skyd Magazine's website in 2011. Lou had already been writing for a year and had developed a small, but cult following. His pieces were sporadic but always gems, yielding such greats a his How to Cheat to Win series and Ku Fu Throwing. When Lou started writing for us on Skyd, he insisted on aggressive regularity that saw him contribute a new piece every Wednesday for another four years.

Typically, the quality and frequency of our contributors fluctuate over weeks and months, but somehow Lou was able to push himself to maintain a consistent high quality of work. It seemed that whether talking about how spirit of the game had evolved at the elite level or detailing different team cultural approaches, Lou was always good for at least one epiphany-type moment that made you see ultimate (and often life) in a new light.

What I loved the most about Win the Fields was that its focus ranged widely. When a topic would come up in the world of ultimate, like the rise of professional leagues, Lou would always have something to say, some angle of approach.

On a cool fall afternoon, Lou let me know over the phone that it was time for him to move on from Win the Fields to focus on family and his work, teaching for a small school in Oregon. I told him that I was surprised that he was able to keep up his writing for so long. I told him that his words and his curious passion for the sport and its community helped define an era of ultimate and has left a mark for all writing about our sport to examine itself by. Lou thanked me humbly and told me how much a privilege it was to be able to share his thoughts on Skyd. We hung up and I took a moment to reflect in a soft Seattle drizzle.

As you'll see reading through this compendium, Lou's curiosity for ultimate is infectious and fearless. He is constantly seeking the solutions to issues that many of us didn't even realize existed or were afraid to examine.

Win the Fields may not have always had the answers, but Lou always asks the right questions.

Elliot Trotter
Editor in Chief, Skyd Magazine

WIN the FIELDS

1

WHAT'S WINNING THE FIELDS?

On winning the fields

Published Tuesday, July 6, 2010

Winning the fields means being the last carload of people on the fields after a tournament. Since the cag is one of my three favorite things about ultimate and since winning the field often involves several hours of cagging, I love winning the fields.

I talked a little bit about Fugue winning the fields on 97430, but my all time favorite win has to be at Flowerbowl 2002. Mizu and I were freshly and madly in love. Riot beat Schwa in the first final. At that time some of Schwa's players were a bit less than friendly and not particularly well-liked in Vancouver, so the entire crowd was behind Riot the whole way. Then we (the Fish) played Furious in the second final and the crowd was against us the whole way. It didn't matter; the Vancouver crowd is one of the best in ultimate: knowledgeable, enthusiastic and partisan so it's great to have them cheer against you. We beat the Monkey. At home.

HOW CAN YOU NOT LOVE SOMEONE WHO WANTS TO WIN THE FIELDS?

After about twenty minutes of slapping hands and visiting, I turned to Mizu and said, "What do you think about winning the fields?" She said, "Great." How can you not love someone who wants to win the fields after they've already been sitting around watching ultimate for two-and-a-half hours? We cagged around and visited with the Canadians (mostly Al Bob.) We tried to hit the storage box two fields away with oranges (Giora hit it.) We hacked, played reindeer games (Muck Around) and threw. Finally, even the tournament director was left and the sun was going down, so we decided to roll out.

Rather than go home, we went down into Vancouver and got slabs for dinner. We sat outside on the street and watched the world walk by. Then we got gelato. Then cupcakes. Then we went down to the water and watched the last of the light fade out of the day (which June 10th in Vancouver is about 10:30 PM.) When darkness had fallen and the sunset watchers had given way to bonfires and drunken dancers, we strolled back to our car and started the drive home to Seattle.

That's winning the fields.

2

GET IN THE BACK OF THE LINE

On why refs are a bad idea

Published Wednesday, February 9, 2011

Right now, ultimate is in the front of the line. A line of one, but we're in the front. As soon as we add referees at any division of the sport, we move to the back of the line. Behind soccer, rugby, lacrosse, rowing, tennis, wrestling...you name it. In case you haven't noticed, resources are incredibly scarce out there right now. Even sports on the big time are struggling. As we consider these issues, we should consider where we are, where we are going and how we can best get there.

Right now, under SotG, our sport is growing at a breakneck pace. We are outgrowing soccer, lacrosse, rugby...you name it. This is absolutely fantastic. There is nothing that will help our sport more right now than growth. A big part of that growth it SotG and self-officiation. Most of our growth is coming in the youth division and parents love SotG and the culture it brings to our sport. The moral lessons inherent in ultimate and SotG are ones that every parent wants to teach their kid: respect, restraint and honesty. Not only that, the culture of ultimate is a welcome respite from the nastiness of high-stakes soccer or basketball. At the core of that culture is SotG. Every game you play, SotG helps build that respect and culture. To be able to say to a parent, "Ultimate is self-officiated at all levels," is incredibly powerful.

Club and college ultimate should serve as banner divisions to promote the growth of our sport. As such they should do so within the framework of SotG. It kind of goes back to If it Ain't Broke... We are growing at a torrid pace with SotG at all levels. Why would we change it? As a brief aside, both the college division and the club division need some changes to function better. The Open College division needs to make some changes in the way games are observed to prevent the kind of debacle we saw in the finals last year. Less time for discussion, TMFs for every bad call and censuring of coaches. The Club division needs to get out of Sarasota and out of October. Please! Who watches those games? Put the finals in Boston or Seattle where you will have 10,000 fans and youth players watching.

Now that I've distracted you from my main point, let me conclude in a high quality, middle school conclusion kinda way. The most important element for the development of our sport right now is growth. We are currently growing at the fastest rate of any sport in the country and we are doing it with SotG functioning at all levels. Not only should we keep SotG at all levels, we should strengthen the presentation of it at the Club and College levels so they can serve as flagships for the sport.

3
THE POWER OF A NAME

On team names

Published Friday, April 15, 2011

A conversation I had this week got me thinking about the power of names...

Following a disappointing season in 1998 (including the nastiest dirt road ever) and several years of internal acrimony (several posts in its own right), Sockeye fell apart. Eight guys, mostly older, left to join up some Rhino and NYNY guys to make the super-whore-team Blaze of Glory. Those of us who were left set out to pick up the pieces. It was clear right away that the team was going to be nothing like it had been in the past. Whole sections of the offense (Shekky, Tommy, Federbush) had left and big chunks of the d-team's ability to score (Keith Monohan, Ricky Mel, Gary Brady, Jonny G) had gone too. We were a new team.

We recognized we were a new team and planned for a new name. I can remember sitting around in the Jaded House and throwing around possible names: Emerald City, Pod, who knows what all else. Nothing seemed any good. Finally after two weeks of one idiotic name after another, we gave up and became Sockeye again.

Immediately, the expectations and attitude of the team changed. We weren't some young, dumb upstart team anymore we were Sockeye! We were legit! We were contenders! (We weren't really, but that's not the point.) When we kept the name, we kept all the expectations. We kept the attitude. The three consecutive trips to finals in 95, 96 and 97? Ours. World Gold medal in 97? Ours.

Without the name would Seattle have still turned into the dominant team it was 2004-2008? Maybe. But maybe not. There is no way we would have won without the return of all the great Seattle juniors players (Nord, Chase, CK...), who at one point made up a third of the team. I know that a big pull for them was to play for Sockeye. Not Seattle necessarily, but Sockeye. All through those dark years of 99-03 (which Roger and I still call the Dark Years), we were buoyed by our expectations. By our Sockeye expectations. We kept chipping away at our inadequacies until we met and surpassed what had been.

Names have power. They carry with them the weight and strength of past achievements and expectations. That's why I get a little smile every time I see that Ring is still Ring and Chain is still Chain and the Lady Condors are still the Lady Condors. That's why I mourn a little for the loss of a team like DoG or Godiva or NYNY or Windy City.

4
MAKING IT

On trying out

Published September 7, 2011

With Labor Day weekend in the rear view mirror, most of us (including me) are heading back to school and the beginning of school brings the college try-out season. As someone who got cut in my first tryout for Carleton (in 1991) and nearly cut in my first tryout for Sockeye (in 1996) I've always had sympathy for those people grinding it out on the bubble. So here's what you need to do to make it…

1. Be fit. The horse is almost out of the barn on this one, but it isn't entirely too late. If you aren't fit, at some point you will tire. When you tire, you will falter. When you falter, you will make mistakes. Do I need to go on? Michelle Akers said, "Your own fitness is the only thing you control." So control it.

2. Throw within yourself. The most common mistake tryouts make is throw beyond their ability. There's no surprise here; most tryouts are coming from another team (high school, b team, second team) where they have had to be The Man. If you are trying out for a team, though, you're not The Man. (If you're going to be The Man on your new team, you can ignore all of this advice except the last piece.) Throwing in a tryout isn't about being a great thrower or even completing all your passes. It's about demonstrating to the team that you understand yourself as a thrower and can play within that. Can't throw at all? No biggie. Just catch and then hand it off immediately to a handler; they'll love you. No forehand? Don't sweat it. Just fight for that backhand every time.

3. Play defense. Every team in the world has a place for someone who can play nasty defense. If you can't play defense, the tryout committee will be arguing about where they might be able to fit you. If you can play defense, they'll be arguing about how they are going to use you.

4. Play to your strengths. Whatever you are good at, you should do. Whatever you are bad at, you should hide. Hiding your weakness is a great skill. You'd be surprised how many great club players are actually terrible at some aspect of the game, but are functionally okay at this weakness just by hiding it. I will contradict myself here a bit and say that if you are trying to make a team as a thrower, you will need to take some chances and make big throws. If you're good, you'll hit them, too.

5. Don't be a jerk. , the coaches and captains are charged with making

the best decision for the team. I have seen lots of good players get cut, just because they were jerks. From the outside and from the point of view of whoever got cut, this is totally unfair. Here is a tryout, clearly talented enough to make the team, cut for personal reasons. Seems messed up right? It isn't, really. A team is more than a cluster of talented people. It has to work and to click and to function together. The wrong combination of people is painful (we've all been on that team) and it is right for the captains and coaches to try to prevent that. As a tryout, you control your own behavior. If you can't say anything nice, don't say anything at all. (And don't call any travels!)

Good luck.

5
FLAWED PLAYER, FLAWED SYSTEM

On self officiation

Published September 20, 2011

If you spend any time reading rec.sport.disc, you quickly run into Toad Leber. Aptly nicknamed, Toad is widely reviled as one of the greatest trolls on a message board full of trolls. However, if you look through the vitriol, bad language and ad hominem attacks, you will find a genuine and solid foundation to his arguments. Not a foundation I agree with, but one that should be taken seriously and considered carefully.

My purpose here is to look at the ideas, not the man, but an examination of Toad's career and philosophy will help shed light on the argument itself. The development of his ideology is well documented in Leonardo's First 40 Years. What is detailed there is no different from the experiences of so many ultimate players. Players begin with a naive sense of Spirit of the Game that assumes all will accept its premise and play fairly. Then, an encounter with a team or individual who cheats, abuses/uses the rules or otherwise violates that naive sense of Spirit of the Game. Finally, a realization that it is possible (even easy) to cheat and get away with it. All ultimate players come to this crossroads. For Toad, this moment came courtesy of his hero, Kenny Dobyns. Ironically, my own denouement was thanks to UNCW and ECU as Carleton floundered to a 1-4 record against them at College Nationals (92-95). For many players, their experiences at this crossroads begets a belief in the Flawed Player, Flawed System theory of SotG. This is the foundation at the heart of Toad's arguments.

The Flawed Player, Flawed System argument runs like this: in a self-officiated game, it is possible to cheat without penalty. Players are morally flawed and will cheat. Therefore, the system is broken and should be changed to a referee system. Each of these three statements demands a close examination both for their validity and their assumed implications.

The first of these statements does not look deeply enough. It should more accurately say "it is possible to cheat without on-field penalty." Until you've experienced the snub at the tournament party, the muttered disrespect from other players and the awkward silences of your friends and teammates you should be careful about saying that there is no penalty. In a community as small as ultimate's, these off-field penalties are a powerful force and shouldn't be underestimated. While I was working on this post, I was reading the Krakken's article about the differences between ultimate in the States and in Europe and struck by this comparison: "In the Netherlands there is a lot of down time at tournaments where you just hang out and watch games. This time is scarce at American tournaments. Because of all of this, there is less interaction with opponents and more focus on your own team." Does this increased community time increase the strength of these off-field penalties and with them adherence to SotG? Does this partially help explain why SotG is so much stronger in Club ultimate where everyone knows everyone else, than in College where turnover is so fast? But realistically, there are people who are unmoved by these pressures.

Let's look at the second statement. Sure, people are flawed. I don't think is a new idea. But they aren't flawed all the time. Time and time again in ultimate, you will see players in intense and difficult situations doing the right thing. I'm not talking about the things you notice, like receivers retracting a call made in the heat of the moment. I'm talking about all the catches, throws, d-blocks and goals that pass by without any call or drama. Even when calls are made, it is easy to forget the marker graciously accepting the foul call from the thrower or a handler laughing at a travel call because they know how bad they walked. Even when we notice, we forget these things. If you are trying to evaluate how flawed people are, you can't look only at the bad.

I'm not sure where to start with the third statement. The leap of logic is amazingly magnificent and unjustified. There are hidden assumptions here that need discussion. The first is the idea that since SotG is flawed, it must be replaced. Refereeing is not a perfect system either. In the Flawed Player, Flawed System argument, there is no attempt to consider the relative benefits and drawbacks of each system. No attempt to weigh each system side-by-side. It is simply, Spirit is flawed and must go. The other hidden assumption is that officiating is the only issue of importance to ultimate and all decisions about officiating should be made within this framework. Growth? Juniors? Image? Community? Legitimacy? These are not small, unimportant details to be brushed aside. The effect of SotG and refereeing on these and other issues is essential to the debate about the future.

To be fair, the initial premises of the Flawed Player, Flawed System theory have real validity. As a critique of SotG, they really get to the heart of the issues. It is possible to cheat. People do cheat. A robust Spirit of the Game would address those issues head on. For the most part, we have avoided those issues, preferring to be reactive rather than proactive. What does proactive mean? What does proactive look like? A final thought, without a home elsewhere in this essay is that the Flawed Player, Flawed System theory can become a self-fulfilling prophecy. In a corrosive cycle, it becomes a rationale and justification for the very behavior it decries.

6

DEFENDER'S MENTALITY

On defense

Published September 26, 2011

A few years back I started playing city league soccer with a bunch of Sockeye guys. I had played as a kid and though I loved it, I drifted away. I ran track in high school before finding ultimate in college. All those 25 years of sports, from the time I was 5, I had played defense. So when I went to playing city league soccer, I was surprised to find that I was a much better striker than a defender. There were some technical reasons (I had speed, but no ability to head the ball, etc.) but mostly it was mentality. There was something similar between striking in soccer and defending in ultimate.

Mia Hamm wrote, "I am a goal scorer and rarely are goal scorers successful. If it is only when [you score] you gain confidence, you are going to be miserable." Defending in ultimate is also about failure. You can play the best, most technically sound defense in the world and still look like a fool. That constant drumbeat of defeat can be crushing and powerfully motivating at the same time. The trick is to carry the defeat with you and at the same time nurse a prodigious ego. That's why defenders looked pissed off all the time; their psyches are split in half and hating each other.

There is something too about taking chances. Playing defense, particularly once you become good at playing off-man, is about chances. When Sockeye plays zone d, the criteria for success is one good bid each point. Not a block, but one bid. It isn't the block, but the opportunity for one that makes a good defender. Can you, through your vision and creativity, manufacture the possibility of a turnover? This is identical to the goal-scorers mentality. Yes, you want the goal (just like you want the block), but a good opportunity is a measure of success as well. Goals, like blocks, are rare. There comes a time in both soccer and ultimate when opportunities become wasted and creativity needs some blue-collar finishing, but it is the set-up that makes the mindset.

So when I am up in Burlington this weekend watching NW Regionals, I will watch the team strategies and the drama of the tournament, but for individual play it will be the defenders I will watch. The grind and the hustle. The flash and block.

7
A TALE OF TWO STORIES

On Sockeye losing at Regionals

Published October 5, 2011

I was in Burlington this past weekend to watch NW Regionals. A better journalist would have followed the main action and the main story line; I followed my heart. I went to watch Sockeye qualify and to support the Oregon women who were playing for Further. Somehow that got mixed up.

Sockeye and Further's situations in the tournament were weirdly similar. Both were in a cluster of equally good teams vying for the final spot for Nationals. In Sockeye's case they were fighting against Furious and Rhino. For Further, it was Zeitgeist (Bay 2), Schwa and Underground (Seattle 2). But expectations for each team were very different. Sockeye was going to have to work, but would qualify. It didn't even occur to Further (or anyone else) that they were in the running to go.

Much will be made of Sockeye's tactical failures and the execution errors that led to their downfall. This is as it should be. The beautiful clarity of 2010 Sockeye's vertical stack, a clarity that opened up deep lanes for handlers and cutters alike, was gone. In its place was a confused, muddy mess where too often, open players were covered by their poorly spaced teammates. Their handlers settled for easy, rinky-dink resets that got a new 10, but failed to open up throwing options downfield. And Sockeye's stars played poorly, particularly in the fourth quarter of each game, gifting far too many easy goal scoring opportunities to Furious and Revolver. Why did these things happen?

The Fish were a team without identity. The brash, take-no-prisoners attitude of the previous year was gone. It is a tough attitude to maintain two years in a row, particularly in the face of increased expectations. In 2010, no one expected a thing of Sockeye, but after World's silver and Nationals semifinals the belief within and without the team is that they were title contenders. Not that they would contend, but were contenders. This seemingly semantic difference is everything to a team's attitude. Being a contender is something you are. Contending is something you do. When contending is your attitude, fight and struggle is built into what you are.

Sockeye hadn't clearly defined roles and responsibilities for individual players. Throughout the tournament, Sockeye continued to mess around with their roster and playing time. Individual playing time, especially for the bottom 20 or so players fluctuated wildly. Nord didn't play the last 5 points against Furious on Saturday. Montague didn't play at all, but then played 5 against Revolver. Karlinsky emerged from the bottom of the handler rotation to play serious minutes in their Sunday loss to Furious. In August, this is great. You can see who is stepping up and how the pieces will fit together. In October, that work should be done. Everyone should know their role and be able to accurately predict how many points they will play and under what circumstances. Lacking a role and a defined responsibility, an individual player has nothing to be accountable for. No job description to fulfill. Without a clear mission, there is no way to be successful and more importantly, no need to be successful.

The size of Sockeye's roster (27) wasn't doing them any favors, either. I know a huge team is great for practice, but are you really trying to win practice? Is that your goal for the season? The problems of team and individual identity I outlined above are compounded by too many players. The best roles are ones that fit the individual and fit together across the team. This is why teams split O and D. It is easier to define roles and fit them together with a group of 10 than a group of 20.

Much will be made of Ben Wiggins' departure. I don't think the team fretted about it too much, feeling like they had the talent to absorb the loss (and they did). But what was missed wasn't on-field talent, but off-field confidence and certainty. When I played with Ben we often didn't see eye-to-eye on tactics, but 100% tactical perfection doesn't matter. What matters is certainty, clarity, vision and above all, confidence. This was missed.

Further is a team built in a funny gray area between the total, life-absorbing commitment of Sockeye and the no-commitment of a team like Vagabonds (who won Mixed). Coming from a small market (Eugene), there aren't 20 women (or even 10) who are willing to commit the time, money and energy to a full club season. The team is a mix of young, ambitious players (mostly from the U of O) and older players (mostly from city league). For the most part, they come together and play because they love to play and want to play women's.

Going to Regionals there was no expectation for this team that they would make or even contend for Nationals. They only had 13 players. The chalk was that Zeitgeist and Underground would be playing for the last spot. Further was just going to play.

With that attitude in hand, the Eugene women were unfazed by the beating Riot put on them in Round 2 (3-13). Unburdened, they walked over to their all-important game against Zeitgeist. And they won. Scratching and clawing, they pulled out the 11-10 win. At this point in the tournament, they were still very dependent on three stars (McDowell, Craley and Sharman) to carry them, but that would change.

Day 2, they again stared awful defeat in the face, this time at the hands of Traffic (6-15, but they started the game 0-5) in the 3-4 game. Laughing, they shook it off and prepared for the game-to-go against arch-rivals, Schwa. If I might digress for a moment, one of the greatest delights in ultimate is to go to a tournament with a small team, a team you don't know well, not even a team, and over the course of seven games meld and blend and merge until you are a team. This is what had happened to Further. They only played 11 women in the game-to-go, but each of those women knew what her role was and performed it without thought and with the utter confidence that comes with thoughtlessness. The odd thing is, there wasn't much discussion within the team of who should do what. Each player gravitated toward what they did best in combination with what the team needed. The game was tight at half (8-6), but behind blocks from Karpelowitz, Hirsch and Mahoney (all coming off of the bench) Further won going away (15-8).

A last thought. Sockeye went to Regionals looking not to lose. Further went to Regionals looking to play.

8
HOW TO BEAT REVOLVER

On beating Revolver

Published October 19, 2011

Revolver is the putative favorite to win this year in Sarasota. As defending champs, they are sitting on a 33-1 record (with that loss well avenged) and are peaking at the right time. Current spreads have them as a 3.5 point favorite (or better) over every other team in the field. What will it take to stop them?

Disclaimer: read on at your own peril. Other people's scouting reports are notoriously unreliable and I've been badly burned a few times by trusting a report without verifying it for myself. Usually, a report is a good place to start with your own observations. What it comes down to is that you can scout a team, but to beat a team you have to scout the interaction between your team and your opponent.

Revolver is a team with three major components: a stifling man-to-man defense, a possession offense and Beau Kittredge.

Revolver's offense is a clean side-vertical with a slow reset tempo that focuses on an isolated cutter in the lane. They are not risk takers by temperament (except Watson) and will gladly dump-swing-comeback all the way down the field. Actually, that's what they want to do. They don't want to huck it. Hucks are too low-percentage and the Revolver players would rather take the 99% than risk a deep shot. Beau fits into this by providing a free, wide-open reset off of the back of the stack. Teams and individual defenders don't want to be embarrassed by Beau and so they back him. This may help an individual defender's stats ("He never scored on me") but is detrimental to the implementation of an effective team defense.

At the elite level, defense isn't about stopping another team (you can't) but rather forcing them into uncomfortable situations where they will make 4 or 5 more mistakes than usual. Jon Gewirtz of NYNY taught me, "you make them beat you with their weakness. If they do, you make them do it again because it's their f– weakness." In Revolver's case, this weakness is taking chances. Front Beau. Take away those easy resets and force the deep look. Will Beau humiliate you once or twice? Of course. That's part of being a defender.

Additionally, Revolver's side stack is very vulnerable to poaching. The art of poaching off of a vertical stack has disappeared in the last decade as most teams have switched to playing some form of a spread offense, but the possibility of it is as strong as always. Here's how it works. The defender in the lane plays standard fronting defense, denying the comeback. The last back in the vertical stack drifts 10 yards off. This is delicate. You want to be far enough off to be able to reach a deep cutter, but not so far off that the other team blows up their offense into anti-poach mode. Ideally, you can sucker them into continuing to try to run their offense like usual, all the while ensuring it won't. When the players in the stack eventually realize they are being poached, that vertical stack will start to disintegrate as poached cutters move to get the disc. Fortunately, you already have two lanes (deep and outside-comeback) covered. The third lane (inside-comeback) is covered by a switching defender from the interior of the stack. The far side of the field is covered by the stack and its defenders. Essentially, you are running a triangle outside, deep and inside with the inside defender pulling off only if necessary.

As good as Revolver's offense is, dealing with their defense is a much more difficult task. They are in the fortunate position to be able to put out seven defenders who are as fast or faster than the seven players on the offense. Additionally, their handler defenders are exceptionally quick and all their defenders are very fundamentally sound with their positioning. These tools enable them to play honest, man-on defense with little or no separation. They are able to bring intense pressure on comeback cuts and resets, thereby taking away the easy pieces of offense. You can score on this unit through the front door, but only if you are spot-on perfect and maintain intense concentration. To maintain for 15 points is unlikely. Better to find an easy way to score.

A classic way to relieve defensive pressure is to break the mark. Against Revolver, break the mark on the inside. Breaking around, which facilitates advantageous field position and sets the thrower up for a great continue, is useless against Revolver. Their defensive speed and technique mean that they are recovering into position on the mark and downfield quickly enough to prevent a continuation. Breaking inside has two advantages. An inside break gains yards. Also, insides are so much quicker than arounds that the marker and defnders have little time to react before the new thrower can move the disc downfield.

While Revolver has speed, quickness and technique, they are not big. Several of their main defenders (Kawaoka, Kanner and Sherwood among others) are not tall. A big line up will put pressure on these defenders in the air. Revolver is smart about assignments, both through choices on the line or through playing zone for numbers. This means that their smaller defenders are used on handlers, increasing their effectiveness and limiting their exposure. To take advantage of size mismatches, you need to have the offensive flexibility to send handlers deep effectively.

To put all these ideas together into a winning game plan will require that it fits within your team's game. As effective as a strategy may be, if your team can't implement it, it is worthless.

9

WAIT? WHAT WAS THAT SCORE?

On throwing games

Published October 26, 2011

Regionals and Nationals is the season for throwing games. Thrown games at Regionals and Nationals?! Not every team is trying to win. At Regionals, some teams are content to lose so long as they qualify for Nationals. At Nationals, some teams are happy to just make quarters or the play-in game. The tournament formats are also inefficient. In a pool play format, teams play more games than are necessary to pick a winner. (Single elimination is most efficient.) I'd like to look at how teams will throw games and what the advantages and dangers are. (Here's the Nationals format if you want a look.)

REST YOUR INJURED PLAYERS

This is standard practice for the top teams at the end of the day on Friday in the 1v2 games. While there is some advantage to going into the bracket as the 1-seed (typically, you face an exhausted 4-seed), 1-seeds do lose sometimes (Ring 2004, Sockeye 2008). However, every team at this point in the season and tournament has important players nursing serious injuries. These players don't play in this game.

PLAY AN EVEN ROSTER

This strategy is to preserve energy. Nationals is without question the most grueling tournament in ultimate. The weather is punishing, the teams are all brilliant and the level of play intense. It is to survive this tournament that club teams have such massive rosters. Playing even does two things for a team. First, it rests the legs of your starters, particularly on defense. Second, it gets playing time for a huge number of your bench players. The classic team to do this would be Goat. They play Revolver in the first round (a probable loss) and then a huge matchup with Bravo in the second. The winner of the Goat-Bravo game is probably making the power pool and the loser down into the S-Box. This strategy works; I've been the victim of it. It makes me nervous though, to start a tournament not playing your best. It becomes a real test of your mental ability and strength.

SIT YOUR STARTERS

Although all kinds of teams use this strategy at Regionals, it is very unlikely that a men's team will employ this at Nationals. This is a very good strategy when teams are extremely unbalanced. On the men's side, this situation doesn't exist too much. On the women's side, however, it is quite likely that a 2- or 3- seed would bench their starters against a 1-seed like Fury or Riot. Physically, it makes sense.

There is a big drop off (although it is narrowing) between the top few teams and the second level. Those second level teams are typically dependent on a handful of players for success and resting them keeps them fresh over a long weekend. Psychologically, it is a bit dicey. You aren't playing your best. (Ugh.) You are creating an internal division between stars and not-stars. (Ugh.) I have seen this work (painfully) and fail (even more painfully.) It is a very risky strategy.

IMPLEMENTATION

The benefits of throwing games are largely physical and the dangers psychological. Managing the implementation of these strategies can preserve the former while mitigating the latter. Should you consider these, I would avoid team-wide discussions. Prepare as always, even people who might not be playing. (Injured players aside.) A very successful implementation is the 'decide at half' technique. Down 3-8? Bench the starters. Up 8-6? Go for it! Gradations of these strategies are also quite good. Play your starters a half or a quarter of their usual points. Realistically, all of these strategies fail more often than they succeed, no matter how well they are implemented. Quite simply, teams chose to use these risky strategies because they need to. If they were more likely to win, they'd just step up and play.

10
REFLECTIONS

On 2011 Nationals

Published October 26, 2011

I've stumbled back from Sarasota with a head full of thoughts and ideas and impressions. I went as a broadcaster working on the NexGen live feed, so while I spent my time mostly focused and working, my spectation wasn't coherent; I just watched what was in front of me (which is what I was announcing). Correspondingly, here are my thoughts in no particular order.

THE GREAT

The two most impressive performances I saw were from Alex Snyder (of Fury) and the entire Revolver D team. Alex's forehand was the difference in the finals. Her ability to use it to cut through the wind and find the high side of the field was crucial to Fury's 5-point run that spanned halftime. (From 4-4 to 9-4.) Equally masterful was her performance in the semifinals against the Capitals where she threw at least 4 beautiful hucks, shelfing them out for the receivers to run on to. It was impressive enough upwind, but that two of them were completed downwind with touch was masterful. It's also hard to say enough about the Revolver defense. Having gotten a really great look at it across 2+ games, I've come to realize that as technically sound as the downfield work is, it is the marking that is truly exceptional. In the finals versus Ironside, the Revolver marks were able to keep the boys from Boston pinned on the forehand side, allowing their defenders to hone in and sell out on stopping comeback cuts into the hole. Even when Ironside was able to hit arounds or comebacks, the mark was established immediately, disrupting any flow (particularly east-west.)

THE SAD

I was generally disappointed in the lack of sophistication displayed by many of the teams, particularly the open teams. In both open games I watched in their entirety (DW vs Goat and Revolver vs Ironside), the losing team failed to adjust their strategy despite steadily falling behind. In both games, the losing teams played man, got scored on and played more man. Goat didn't force a turnover from the DW offense until something like 13-8. In their first eight defensive points of the final, Ironside played man seven times and forced one turnover. In their one point of zone/junk, they forced two. What did they play on their ninth defensive point? You guessed it: man-to-man. I understand that changing strategies out of desperation is risky and that the best way to win is to stay true to your nature as a team, but why not build a team identity that is flexible? Why not anticipate the need to play zone or junk in addition to man-to-man. Also, if you get in a game and realize that you are on a path to defeat, why not try another path? Even if it is a risky gamble, why would you rather stay with a sure loser. Would you rather guarantee a 10-15 loss or risk a 7-15 loss with the small possibility of victory?

THE STRONG

Riot's comeback in the face of sure defeat showed admirable resilience. The opportunity lost when a swing pass to Jinny Eun floated a titch too high and too long decided the game. During that final stretch of points, Fury's conditioning was beginning to flag. Their cutters where stagnant and their defenders were reacting rather than anticipating. I'm guessing Matty Tsang recognized this as well; he played a surprisingly second-string line late in the game (I believe at 14-12) to rest his stars as best he could. Oh, but that turn. And only 10 yards out of the Fury endzone. Alas for Riot. But put that aside a moment and ask this about Riot: what did they accomplish? After two disappointing collapses in back-to-back semifinals, Riot stared themselves in the mirror and saw that their greatest weakness was their mental game. Acknowledging their weakness, Riot set out to overcome it. I don't know all the details of how exactly they built their mental strength, but you don't pull yourself out of a 13-8 hole without a good deal of resilience.

THE LAY OF THE LAND

While the teams have shifted a bit, the general structure in the men's and women's divisions hasn't changed much in the last decade or so. On the open side, there is one dominant team (Revolver), handful of semis-caliber teams (DW, Ironside, Chain and Sockeye) and a gaggle of teams fighting to rise into and above quarters (Ring, Goat, Bravo, Furious, Rhino, Southpaw, Machine, Truck, etc, etc.) Just as the worst bullying in middle school is among the middle of the social pack kids, the nastiest battles are between the teams fighting to move up from quarters to semis. On the women's side, there are two great teams (Riot and Fury) one of whom always beats the other when it counts. Behind them are a pack of teams fighting for a spot in semis (Phoenix, Molly Brown, Scandal, Capitols, Showdown and Traffic) and behind them another pack of teams looking to knock them off and make quarters (Nemesis, Brute, Ozone, etc, etc.) Is this going to change? Maybe. How will it change? With Matty likely to sign on for another Worlds year, Revolver in its prime and Riot on the upswing, it doesn't look like the three teams perched at the top (Revolver, Fury and Riot) are going to get any worse, so it will be a matter of some other teams moving up. Ironside is in a good spot. If they can figure out how to get Stubbs in a more central offensive role (instead of brilliant role player) and patch up some of their deficiencies at the handler spot, they should be in position to step forward without major changes. DW and Chain both look like teams that are at the end of their strategic paths and in need of reinvention to take a step forward. In particular, DW will need to get over the exultation of finally being able to destroy bad and mediocre teams (of which they were one not so long ago) and start figuring out how to beat good teams consistently. On the women's side, the payout from the '06 junior worlds team and the '10 college season just keeps on going all over the country. To compete with Riot and Fury, however, the young players on these teams are going to have to figure out how to be great in a hurry. One (or more) of these teams will pull this off.

THE ADJUSTMENTS

There are a few nagging details from both finals that I have to mention. First, Riot's tactics against Fury's zones and junk. Riot consistently had all six of their receivers within 15 yards of the disc. Even when they broke through, they had nowhere to go. A fundamental element of the Condor's zone strategy (the originators of the 2-handler set) is to spread out so that once you beat the cup, you have a numerical advantage downfield. Also, I thought that Riot was lacking a dominant throwing handler. O'Malley, Weatherford and Eun are all cutting handlers, doing most of their damage with their legs. Clemens and Ambler are solid and dependable. Of the two players I would consider for this spot, Titcomb and Suver, the former was out for the year with an ACL and the latter has yet to find the consistency at the club level she displayed in college. A last note on breaking zones. There are four ways to beat a zone: in, through, around and over. Riot used three of the four, but failed to utilize overs with any meaningful results. This falls squarely on the lack of a throwing handler; it is her job to deliver overs consistently regardless of the weather. Looking at Ironside's offense, their inability or refusal to move the disc to the weakside killed them. Yes, Revolver's marks are superb, but they are still breakable and must be broken. Systematically, there are two ways to accomplish this: play off tempo (throwing the dump on stalling 1,2,3) or losing more yards to gain space. To run the vertical offense that Ironside wants to use, you must be able to dump-swing, regardless of what the other team is doing defensively.

THE BRILLIANT

The best two plays I saw all weekend both came courtesy of Revolver. The first, from Jon Levy, came on Revolver's first defensive point of the finals. Off of the pull, Ironside centered to Rebholz. After some initiating motion, Rebholz had a cutter free coming down the center, but definitely on the open side. Rebholz hit him with the easy forehand. Actually, he didn't. Anticipating and timing his dive perfectly, Levy left his force backhand position to fully layout and cleanly block the disc. A couple passes later, it was 2-0 Revolver. The second was the layout goal by Sherwood. The thrower didn't do him any favors, launching a chest-high bullet that turned over and died as quickly as it could toward the grass. Maintaining a half step on Stubbs, Sherwood tore down the field as and somehow got to the disc just before it was down.

THE WEST IS THE BEST

Capped by Further, the NW women's teams finished 1, 2, 5 and 9. The women from Eugene took only 15 players, none of whom had ever been to Club Nationals before in any capacity. After a disappointing performance the first four rounds (26-60 cumulative), they beat Bent (15-7), RevoLoution (15-13) and then Brute Squad to finish an exultant ninth. Up 12-10 on Brute Squad, they managed to kill the clock with a stultifying zone that ate 20-minutes and the hard cap, so that even when Brute scored the game was over 12-11. Their Nationals ended up surprisingly similar to their Regionals. In both tournaments, they managed to ignore some bad defeats and win all their close games thanks to a small squad that got better at playing together as the weekend went on.

THE BRUTAL

I'm not even talking about the Monkey.

THE NEGLECTED

For now. So much still to talk about that I can't get to. Fury's pick-your-poison offense. The limitations and possibilities of DW's two man game. Surly wins! Surly wins! The ugly last point of the Wheelchair-Beyonders game. Who's the greatest player in ultimate? The promise and possibilities of Riot's offense. Fury's fascination with junk d. Would it work without Liz Penny? The spacing on Revolver's offense. Not their flow, but their pull plays. The mental game. The mental game beyond stilling the mind. All the little oddities I learned about announcing and calling a game and providing color and interviews and all that production stuff. Suits are sweet. I could go on and on and on…

11

2-MAN ZONE O WAS INVENTED IN 1954

On zone O, history

Published November 8, 2011

In my recent write-up on Nationals, I stepped in it with this line: "A fundamental element of the Condor's zone strategy (the originators of the 2-handler set) is to spread out so that once you beat the cup, you have a numerical advantage downfield." This was the second time I had alluded to the 2-man zone offense as the Condors' work and that was more than Jim Parinella could bear. What followed was part history lesson, part discussion, part strategy session as Parinella, then Alex Defrondville (the Count) and finally Steve Dugan all weighed in. The conversation went all over the place; here's the condensed version:

JIM: You can ask the old Condors, they took this directly from us. We played this since at least 1992 or 1993 (i.e., pre-DoG), though it was probably 1994 when we really started pushing the wings downfield. And we had to get it from somewhere. Did NYNY do something like this too?

ME: My experience as a defender is that the trio (playing in pairs) of Studaris, Taro and Dugan played this offense differently than any other team I'd seen. In particular, their willingness to play their handlers close together seemed new and innovative. I played the two handler set with Sockeye (learned it from Jonny [Gewirtz of NYNY]) but we spread the handlers.

JIM: I am watching the 1994 semis. The critical elements of the two handler set are: a) no dump-swing. The first look after the dump is often right back to the dumper b) no "popping". The poppers work the area behind and to the side of the middle middle, sliding around in that area. c) deep wings. This creates space for the poppers and gives the option of the hammer. [Lou's note: Jim also sent me a great article he had written a while ago that hopefully can be made available.]

COUNT: I think NY definitely did a little of the two handler set, based on Danny Weiss pushing the disc, similar to what Boston did with me. But they didn't do it exclusively like we did. We definitely always focused on losing as little space as possible on the dump. [Another] rationale behind the close dump is based on the number of dump/ long swing turnovers that occur. Our 2 handler zone O was actually based on having the defenders stationary, not trying to take advantage of seams opened by having the zone in motion. Far safer to identify the open receivers and deliver based on a stationary defender than to

lose track of a defender while the zone was in motion.
STEVE: The Condors did get the idea from DoG. The main part we added/developed was the handler catching short passes moving forward into the cup. This gave the handler vision of the field while putting him closer to the gaps in the cup.

LOU: This is the piece that really identifies the Condor system and distinguishes it from previous 2-handler sets.

STEVE: The other concept was the one man advantage upfield. 5 on offense vs 4 on defense. We stressed the idea of using that advantage after the handlers got a pass through the cup. We termed it "off to the races". [Lou's note: this is the piece I felt Riot was missing.]

LOU: The advantage of outnumbering the defense was always there [in the 2-handler set], although Sockeye's 2-handler sets in the late 90s [using a 2-post] were much slower and that the outnumbering piece was often limited to the two poppers in the middle of the field, typically Federbush and Ahouse. Steve, did you all put much structure into where the downfield players went? As a defender, I always felt like they were just drifting in an open, unstructured way.

STEVE: We had a 3 popper, 2 deep structure. The deeps stretched the field and stayed toward the sideline. This forced the deep defender to choose a man to cover. As the disc broke through the cup to the poppers, we had 1 deep cut in along the center line while the other deep cut away, usually giving the poppers a short pass to the deep coming in. With the poppers, we stressed just shifting away from defenders while keeping the field spread horizontally. The shifting was just walking away from the defender, not cutting. The key part was keeping space between the poppers so that 1 defender could not cover two poppers. I always thought of it as if the 5 upfield were centers of circular areas and good spacing meant the areas had very little overlap.

COUNT: We [were] definitely looking to go through and/or around. [Lou's note: There was a mistake here in the original text. It should say through and/or over.] What I find disappointing, especially at the highest levels (watching some open points last weekend) is how few people go over, and I'm talking the 10-15 yard hammer/blade to someone who is pretty much wide open. [Lou's note: I totally agree with the Count here.] But as Steve said, the goal was always to get off to the races once we punched it through however we did it.

JIM: We pretty much stopped practicing zone O in about 1997. We still played it when we practiced our zone D, but we didn't really work on anything. Alex would handle, I'd pop, and the others would play off of us.

STEVE: This brings up a very interesting difference between DoG and Condors. DoG had/has very specific people in specific positions and had defined O and D lines. Condors used various people as O handlers and switched up the O and D lines.

At the end of this email conversation, Steve was nice enough to take some time to chat with me over the phone about the development of the Condors' zone offense and share a zone offense and defense drill with me. (See below.) We talked first about the development of the crash-first method of zone offense. Steve wasn't exactly sure on the date, but he said it definitely came after they adopted the 2-handler set from DoG following the Condors' loss in the 98 final. That would be the 1999 season. I remember Studaris victimizing Sockeye in this offense at the first ECC in 2001. Dugan credited Vince Birch with the crash into the cup reset; Vince used it to such a degree against trapping zones that the Condors called this move the "Vince Break." Beyond that, Dugan couldn't really point to a single moment when the crash-first became the Condors' zone o, but he did site Studaris, Taro, Jason Seidler and himself as the main handlers involved. (Condors played open subbing at that time and were much more flexible with assignments than most teams.)

What's all this mean?

The 2-handler set is old as dirt. DoG used it as early as 1992-3 and maybe got it from NYNY. DoG's system was a lose-no-yards system that went around and over. [Lou's note: same mistake here as above. It should say through and over. "We NEVER went around," adds Al.] Sockeye played this system as early as 1996, my first year on the team. Sockeye's system was a slow, 2-post system that went through and around. The Condors began using 2-handlers in 1999 and at some point turned it into the crash-first system so popular today.

Dugan's Drill: First, the goals of the drill. For the defensive wings and deeps: to communicate and work together. For the cup: to recover and reset. For the downfield offensive players. To keep the disc moving quickly (with short, crisp passes.) Now for the set up. Place two lines of cones across the field 6 -10 yards apart. (Adjust distance according to need.) These are dividing lines to section the field. The cup (2 points and a middle) and a handler (with disc) are spread out on the first line of cones. The downfield defenders (2 wings and a deep) and the downfield offensive players (3 middles and a deep) are spread out anywhere they want beyond the second line of cones. The downfield defenders communicate how they will cover. Disc is checked into play with a throw from the handler to whoever is open. Disc is live. The offense will try to keep the disc moving and score. The defense will try to slow play long enough to let the cup recover. If the cup ever gets to "Stall 3" play is dead.

12
TOWARDS A HEALTHY ECOSYSTEM

On modern offensive structure

Published November 16, 2011

The ecology of Ultimate offenses is in a state of flux. After years of horizontal stack monoculture, we are seeing an increase in teams running vertical stack. All four of the finalists on the open side ran variations on vertical stack. The women's finalists both ran horizontal offenses; Fury's quite traditional and Riot's quite new. Our sport is still so young that there are incredible opportunities for invention and creation. There is a constant quest for a 'better' offense. An offense that will be so perfect that it alone elevates its team to a championship. No offense will do that. Revolver won because they are more talented and they execute their system flawlessly. It isn't the system. It is the talent and the execution. The return to vertical stack hints at a new stage in the development of ultimate. A stage where there are a variety of accepted strategies and methods. Each team, based on talent and preferences of leadership, pick and choose what they want to run. Here are the main offensive choices:

STANDARD VERTICAL

The main principles of this offense are dump-swing handler movement, a cutting lane on either side of the stack that allows for in-out cuts. Because of the dump-swing required to access the far side of the field, this offense needs several handlers who can possess and reset the disc consistently. It is a very good system for a college team because it doesn't require much in the way of judgment on the part of the cutters – usually your most inexperienced players. The main weakness is extreme vulnerability to the 'triangle defense.' Ironside runs this offense.

STANDARD HO (CUTTER)

The set up for this offense is two lines of players (handlers and cutters) horizontally across the field. In this variation of the offense, the two central cutters churn for big under cuts and then look to huck it to the two cutters set up on the outside. The handlers stay back and possess the disc, ideally keeping it in the middle of the field. This offense requires very talented 3-cutters. The championship Furious teams who developed and ran this offense had Lugsdin and Grant as their central cutters. The weakness of this offense is how poorly it functions on the sideline. Furious' solution was to run it as a side-stack at this point, but it still struggled on the edges. Fury runs this offense.

STANDARD HO (HANDLER)

Basically the same set up as the cutter version of this offense, but the two stacks are spread out a bit more with the cutters pushed back just a bit. This creates lots of space for handlers to cut up the line and across the front of the disc for leading passes and gut shot passes. These little handler to handler passes open up funny-space shots to cutters moving at angles down-field. You need a crew of good handlers to make this work. They run a lot and they need to be in rhythm with each other. This offense really spreads responsibility, so everyone needs to play near perfect for it to work. If everyone has a merely 'good' day, those turnovers can pile up fast. Riot runs a version of this offense.

SIDESTACK

The plan for this offense is to move all the cutters to one sideline and create a single giant throwing lane on one side of the field. This creates a lot of space for each cutter. It your throwers can break the mark and huck no single defender can win their match up; there's too many options to deal with. The defensive key against this offense is to play help defense and double team the main cutter. The tricky part here is the poaches really become a three man system (cover, poach and clean up) which is complicated and easy to mess up. Still, teams will try it, so if you run this offense you will need to be good at dealing with garbagey defenses. This is Revolver's offense.

SPREAD

The term spread has come to mean any offense that places the cutters across the field in a way that isn't clearly horizontal. The original ('German') version of this offense came to the United States courtesy of Feldrunner Mainz in 1997. Their version featured four handlers back, a single central cutter and two deeps all the way back at the goal line. They would lead off with a space pass to the central cutter and then play 3-on-3 with the handlers coming up from behind. This version needs a great connection between the 2 and the 3; both should be dominant players. The main weaknesses are that it doesn't run well in the wind and doesn't recycle very well; it is hard to make it flow. There are other spread versions, but all are victim to the same major weaknesses. Many teams run these sets as pull plays, but no one uses them as flow.

80S VERT

No dump. Stack a mile long. It's hard to imagine how this offense works, but it does. By pushing the front of the stack away from the thrower, a huge space is created for handlers to work for big lateral swing passes. These swing passes gain yards and position, opening up throwing lanes to the cutters. The weakness is that it is comparatively too easy to shut down the reset, which generates short field turnovers. Seaweed uses these principles in their offense.

FASTBREAK

Based on Nolan Richarson's '40 Minutes of Hell', this offense puts the pedal on the floor and keeps it there. Every time there is a turnover, run and put the disc in play as soon as possible, including sprinting to pick up ob turns and bricks. The tempo of the offense is blinding and the disc should be moved by 3 in the stall count. The idea is to put constant, unrelenting pressure on the other team, generate easy goals and create mental and physical fatigue. The risk is that things can get very, very messy quickly and the turnovers can be really ugly. The other danger is that in a 7-game tournament, you will play 7-games at this pace but your opponents only one. Your conditioning and depth must be fantastic. Fugue 2010 ran this offense.

The subtext to this article has been to encourage you (as coach or captain) to consider the pros and cons of different systems and pick one that is going to work for your team. Just because Revolver or Ironside or Fury or Riot runs a system doesn't mean that it is a good system for your team. Above all, commitment and execution are far more important than a perfect system. Doubt is for the off-season. Once the first practice begins, your focus should be on making what you have work as well as possible.

13
HAM, SWEET POTATO PIE, AND DEFENSE

On modern defensive structure

Published November 23, 2011

Happy Thanksgiving. I am giving thanks for defense, one of my greatest joys in ultimate.

Most teams don't give defensive strategy much thought. It's man-force-forehand and maybe a zone. It's not that these defenses are bad – in fact they can be quite good. It's that there are so many other choices out there and so many other ways to be successful defensively.

Defense is about making the other team uncomfortable. When so many teams play force forehand, everyone gets really comfortable playing against it. You might be a great force-forehand team and a terrible force-middle team, but find force-middle to be far more effective because the other team has never seen it and doesn't know how to attack it. Frankly, I was surprised by how unsophisticated many of the teams at Club Nationals were this year. With teams composed of very experienced players, the opportunity to segregate offense and defense and a need to game plan to beat specific opponents there is no reason for a club team not to be prepared with three or more distinct defenses. The more defenses you can play, the less likely you are to be stuck playing a defense your opponent loves and the more likely you will kryptonite them.

I know these descriptions are thumbnails and each defense merits a full post in its own right. What I want to get at today are the options out there for teams to use so they don't have to be stuck with the same old vanilla defense. Unless they want to be. Vanilla's good.

MAN DEFENSE

FORCE FOREHAND

This is the classic defense of high school, college and city league teams everywhere. It works because most of the people on the other team can't throw forehands nearly as well as their backhands. It also requires very little spatial awareness on the part of the defenders. This defense can get scary-effective in a side wind. Its major weakness is that everyone plays it, so offenses are used to it.

FORCE BACKHAND

At the elite club level, this defense splits time with force forehand. At that level, every team comes equipped with several players who can absolutely rip a forehand. A forehand huck is flatter, faster and less apt to float, making it much harder to defend. Out of necessity, teams force backhand. Another piece of the calculation for these teams is the ease with which teams can throw arounds. Most players are quite good at throwing a backhand around the mark (to reset), but not as good at a forehand. This makes the backhand trap harder to escape. Below the elite club (and a few college teams) level, there isn't much cause to play this defense.

FORCE MIDDLE

This is the greatest defense of all time. Seriously. The only problem is that it requires you to field seven defenders who are fast, technically sound and very good at reading the field. Ideally, all seven can pass the Blindfold Test. (Blindfold Test: magically freeze play and blindfold the defender. Can they point to the other 13 players on the field and say what they are doing?) The advantage is that it overplays the strong side by doubling up the marker and defender. The disadvantage is that defenders can get seesaw-lost and when they do, they get beat badly.

STRAIGHT UP

I've seen this be very effective in games, but not over the course of a season. Usually, it catches a team unawares and they struggle with the constant pressure from the mark. Then they recognize the straight up and that if they just fake once, they can throw whatever they want.

COMBOS AND TRANSITIONS

There are lots of ways to combine these. Straight up for three passes into forehand. Straight up on the sidelines and force forehand in the middle of the field. A progressive trap-to-trap where you trap both sides and play straight up in the middle. And so on. Typically, these are played to stop particular opponents or pull plays. I wouldn't recommend them unless you get to the point of super-flexibility with your defense (see below).

ZONES

3-MAN CUP (DEEPS UP AND BACK) Played with two wings, a short deep and a deep deep, this is the classic zone. The cup's responsibility is to clog the middle of the field and prevent crashes and throughs. If the disc moves to the far side, the cup runs like crazy to get there while the wing and short deep try to avoid getting split. The wings are also responsible for helping the deep deep and often are dropping out into the hammer hole as the disc swings to the far side. A very flexible, but not very aggressive zone.

3-MAN CUP (DEEPS LEFT AND RIGHT)

The cup works the same way, but the big hole is in the middle of the field where the short deep has disappeared from. The wings slide into this gap as the disc moves away from them, vacating the far weak side of the field. This zone is club standard. The big difference is that at the club level, the cups are very skilled at stopping the throughs (so you don't need short deep help) and the throwers are so much more powerful (so the deep deep needs permanent, not occasional help).

3-MAN CUP (TRAPPING VERSION)

It's hard to say if this is a conservative version of a 4-man or an aggressive 3-man. It attempts to combine the best of both. You play 3-man when the disc is in the middle of the field where the offense has so many options and 4-man on the sideline where half the field is a turnover. A more detailed look at the 4-man follows. The problem this zone has is what to do when the disc is 7 yards off the sideline. Do you trap or not here? Also, a smart team will keep the disc away from the sidelines and avoid the trap all together.

4-MAN CUP

This zone brings an extra defender up into the cup allowing the defense to put much more pressure on dumps, swings and resets.

It can trap (force sideline) or not (force middle). For many years following Fury's crushing usage of it in 2003, this was the standard zone defense in women's ultimate. It has always been a part of Florida (the state) ultimate and the Florida connection led Sockeye to use it very effectively this past year. If it is windy enough that you can't throw hammers or the other team just can't throw hammers, this defense is impenetrable. However, if they can throw overs, it isn't so good. One hammer and you're looking at a 3 on 5 the wrong way.

1-3-3

A single defender chases and marks the entire time. A wall of three players, all set at middle-middle depth, stop upfield throws. Two keys for the wall: play on the inside of the marker and don't ever let them throw it between you. The three defenders in the back of zone play a triangle. This is a great beginning zone and is very easy to learn. You can get to good in a single game. Great, of course, takes longer. This zone has also fallen out of favor as more zone offenses crash the cup because the defense isn't really set up to deal with that.

BOX AND ONE

Typically played with a 3-man cup, 2 wings and a deep, the Box and One frees up a defender to play man-to-man on one of the handlers for the other team. This is an absolutely brutal defense against teams that rely on a single thrower. It is a miserable failure against balanced teams.

EXOTICS

There are many more weird zones, but I think their effectiveness can be measured by their longevity.

JUNK

General Note: By junk I mean any defense that lives in the funny place between man-to-man and zone. There is a lot of space between those two types of defense and much of it is unexplored, which is surprising considering how much soccer depends on these techniques.

CLAM

This is a very structured version where every player is assigned a specific area of the field and are responsible for covering (man-to-man) the people who enter it. This defense was originally developed to stop structured vertical stack offenses and did that very well. As vert stack becomes more and more popular, I would expect to see more and more Clams.

FSU

This is a very unstructured defense that tells people to just "do what feels right." You'd be surprised how well it works. Most teams supply some structure to it by sending players in three waves. The first wave is like a cup, the second like wings and the third is your deep(s).

SITUATIONALS

The most obvious situational is to drop the defenders off of the handlers in a flat stack and have them clog the lane. In a vertical stack, the classic situational is to have the deepest player drop off and play 'last back.' These zone pieces, fit inside a general structure of man-to-man, are very effective. To make them great requires that all seven defenders are on the same page and ready to switch.

POACHING

Unfortunately, most teams see this as a defensive lapse and not the incredibly valuable tool that it is. There are always times where your defenders need help with their one-on-ones and there are always times when offensive players aren't doing anything; both of these are great times to poach. As with a Situational, poaching is much more effective when it is a team d and the poacher is supported by timely switches from her teammates.

TRANSITIONS

A transition is where you play one defense for a few passes and then switch to another. Over the years, it has been found to be quite easy and effective to switch from zone to man. Despite occasional efforts, no one has found a use for man to zone. This is a great defense for stopping pull plays and isolations. The drawback is that you don't get to pick your matchups.

HOW TO PICK

A good defensive plan will play a basic man-to-man and a zone defense. This is the minimum. The step up from that (and it is a small one) is to add a junk defense of some kind. The easiest thing to do which will give you three defensive looks off of the pull is to play a man d, a zone and a zone transition. It is quite possible to get to super-flexibility with your defense even as a college team. It is typically a two-year investment to get your team culture up to the standard of playing a bunch of different defenses, but the basic idea is simple. Run a bunch of different zones where the focus is on fundamental zone skills. Run a bunch of different man-to-man defenses where the focus is again on fundamental skills. This will come at a cost of nuanced skills in a particular defense. In your game plan, never play the same defense twice in a row. (Except when you do.) Confusion and uncertainty is major strength of this system. Also, it allows you to find the defense that the other team is terrible at attacking and ride it to victory.

When trying to decide which defenses to pick, familiarity is your best friend. Know how to teach force-forehand? That makes it a good choice. However, if you are trying to run a defense you've never used before the number one trick is patience. The number two trick is patience. Pick a couple fundamental points, hammer those and let the team work through the puzzle of figuring out how to make the defense work. Take the 1-3-3 as an example. Your fundamental points might be that Jeff is your best marker so he will mark and under no circumstances can the disc be thrown through the wall. Right away you will come to some problems: Jeff is getting really tired. The handlers are crashing in front of the wall. Don't let go of your fundamental points, but start solving the problems. Can Jeff use his energy more wisely? Can the wall deal with the crashers without sacrificing integrity?

Good luck. As always, hit me with questions, if you got 'em.

14
CLOWN TENT

On team mentality

Published December 14, 2011

Clown Tent is a team philosophy that shifts the nature of responsibility in an unconventional direction. Clown Tent is incredibly flexible and powerful, but also really dangerous. When it goes wrong, it can go really wrong. When it goes right, though, no team experience is better. Today I want to look at the history of the idea and the philosophical underpinnings of it. Next week, I'll continue with practical applications and questions.

At the beginning of my career as a leader at Carleton (94-95) and extending up through my first stint as captain on Sockeye (98-99) I was very much a devotee of a style of leadership and team philosophy dubbed Brown Shirt. (I know the name is inappropriate, but it got used and stuck.) Simply put, Brown Shirt says 'it's the team way or the highway." The classic example of this is the team that has a very rigid offensive structure without room for individual innovation, creativity or flexibility. You run the cuts as they are designed. End of story. But during my second stint as captain of Sockeye (01-03), that philosophy was put under pressure and eventually gave way to a new idea, the Clown Tent.

In 2002, Sockeye was far from the juggernaut it would become. Since the success of the three silvers in 95, 96 and 97, we had failed to make Nationals twice and even there, never farther than quarters. It was a painful, frustrating experience. In 2002 though, we began to turn the corner. We went to Worlds and finished 3rd, upsetting Jam and Furious to win the bronze. The catalyst for these wins was a defensive squad that was very unconventional; it didn't follow the rules. Much of the credit for this should go to John Hammond. Certainly the most creative defender I ever played with, John would do things that were unexpected and unpredictable. Usually, this would lead to some sort of broken field mess that Roger Crafts and I would try to clean up by poaching, switching and directing traffic. It was incredibly effective, but there weren't clear rules. In describing it to then rookie Giora Proskuroski I said, "John's going to do something crazy, Roger's going to poach, I'm going to try to find the missing guy. You just cover your man." The Friar Tuck of this whole mess was Luke Smith, whose giant white mop would serve as the visual inspiration for the name Clown Tent.

Move forward two years. Looking back, the 2004 championship has an aura of inevitability about it, but at the time it was far from inevitable. The team was still stinging from an awful ending to 2003 (both at Regionals and Nationals) and while we were much more talented (having added starters Chase, Nord, Burkhardt and Keith Monohan), we really struggled to find a cohesion as a team. As late as ECC, the new young talent was considering walking out and making their own team. While we were winning more than we had, it wasn't pretty and it wasn't pleasant. Roger and I had a conversation that had a small part in bringing the team together and a much larger role in the development of the idea of Clown Tent. Prior to 2004, Sockeye had been very hard on each other internally. In mid season, Roger and I decided that wasn't going to work with the new guys and that the two of us in particular were going to have to lay off. We continued to be as hard on each other as ever, but softened our tone with the new guys. Essentially, we started treating each person differently depending on what they needed to be happy and effective.

These experiences (and many others) slowly cohered into the philosophy of Clown Tent which has been one of the foundations of Fugue since 2009. Although the idea is sometimes vague and hard to define, I think it can be described best as a freedom of responsibility. As a player, you are responsible to the team to help it win. How that is going to happen isn't set in stone, but is essential that it does. Another lens is trust. You trust that your teammates are doing the best that they can, while knowing that what they do isn't necessarily going to be what you do. The Clown Tent idea, which initially began on the field, has since spread to the track and the huddle and the van and every element of the team experience. Surprisingly, it has been most powerful completely off the field where it has worked to resolve prickly team dynamics and created a team unified in purpose (if not in action.)

15
CLOWN TENT: SUCCESSES

On success of the Clown Tent philosophy

Published December 14, 2011

This article is part 2 of 4 in a series.

Writing about Clown Tent is tricky. By its very nature, CT is designed to deal with individual idiosyncrasies. On a team where all the players are largely homogenous, are quirk-free or lack creativity, there isn't a need for any type of adjustment or accommodation; CT is unnecessary. The strength of Clown Tent is that it does make exceptions for people and that it builds team unity not through unity of action, but unity of purpose. So a big thanks to the Fugue and Syzygy players who were willing to share their stories.

OREGON FUGUE 2010

After a successful 2009 campaign which saw us bow out in the semifinals to eventual champions UC-Santa Barbara, I was stunned when captain and returning senior Molly Suver told me she was thinking about not playing her 5th year of eligibility. I had known that there was tension between Molly and the team about vision and leadership style, but I was caught off guard by the extent of it. As a captain, Molly wanted to run a very tight ship off the field. Organization, timeliness and focus were very important to her. As anyone who has ever tried to get a team to an 8AM game knows, moving 20 groggy adults can be difficult. While Fugue wasn't the most scattered team I've ever been a part of, they were rather…Eugene. More importantly, the team wasn't very interested in being great in this area; organization just wasn't that important to them. As Molly reflected on it last week, "These factors combined to make interactions with the team stressful and difficult in a lot of situations."

Through the strong encouragement of her teammates, Molly decided to return. She and I talked a lot about what would need to change for both her and the team to be happy. The most obvious difference was that she would no longer be captain. Underlying this choice was a decision to trust the leadership to ensure that the team's flakiness wouldn't affect our on-the-field performance. Molly again: "By being able to relinquish these responsibilities to incredibly capable people, I was able change my own attitude towards the team and the season. Your [Lou's] philosophy of clown tent was pretty instrumental in that change. I realized that I can't change who people are, but I can change how I react to a situation. I can't force people to be on time, but the leadership can make conscious decisions to accommodate different time lines in the morning." One of the biggest changes the team made was adjusting our pregame time management. We acknowledged that this was hurting our performance and that we were incapable of moving quickly. The solution was to build an extra 30 or 45 minutes into our schedule every morning. If we said, "Hotel lobby at 7:10", that was for a 9:00 game only five minutes away. Usually a full van was there and ready to go at 7:10 but there wasn't any stress about the people who were straggling; we had planned for them to be late.

Unlike previous teams (like Sockeye) that had used Clown Tent ideas without the broad philosophy of it, Fugue 2010 explicitly discussed the idea and the implementation. Being out in the open about the team philosophy created an enormous pressure valve. When there was difficulty or stress, often it was cleared up with a laugh and a "Clown Tent." The situation described here were just one of several that the leadership worked on throughout the season. Clown Tent provided a framework that prioritized trust and unity of purpose. This framework was used to resolve and guide any difficulties throughout the season. Molly sums it up nicely: "[Clown Tent] expressed differently [by] each person in their own way. I can say, though, that the whole team became more cohesive, more accepting, more flexible and more intent on our unified purpose. [Italics added.]" Oregon finished the season crushing the competition at Nationals by almost 10 points per game and winning their first title.

CARLETON SYZYGY 2000

In 1999, Carleton lost to Stanford in the finals. It was the second consecutive year Superfly had topped Syzygy for the title and for those of us in blue and yellow it was a painful loss. It was made more painful by the graduation of six brilliant seniors, three of whom (Sharon Goodwin, Jenn Willson and Mizu Kinney) went on to star for Riot and three (SJ Hawley, Cindy Craig and Brooke Harnden) who could have, if they'd chosen that life instead of retiring. Left behind was a crew of tough, physical and athletic defenders but not a lot of offensive talent.

The new team found some success throughout the 2000 season by changing from a ball-control to a huck-and-play-d strategy, but still struggled offensively at key moments. 3-, 4- and 5- turnover points were not uncommon. The stress of this style was compounded by a crew of intensely competitive women. Julia Weese-Young recalls: "I remember that there was drama and that practices where high tension. There was a lot of competitive bullshit. We were pushing hard and pushing each other hard physically and mentally – which was good but some feelings were getting hurt. I remember how strong willed and opinionated all those women were/are. Everyone wanting to make a mark personally, everyone wanting to win too, scared that hard work wouldn't be enough, wanting it so badly."

Things finally reached a head just after Regionals. One of the captains, Paige Anderson remembers, "The meeting was precipitated by a conflict of leadership between the captains (me and Julia) and the other dominant personalities on the team, namely Liz [Penny] and Mimi [Frusha]. You (and potentially me and Jules, as well) had realized that the leadership battle could negatively affect the team if we didn't figure out how to make it all work."

So two weeks before Nationals, when the focus should be on fine tuning and healing, six of us including myself, Julia, Paige, Liz, Mimi and captain Anna Coldham met to clear the air. My goal as coach was to try get these incredibly mentally strong players, all of whom wanted to win so bad, to quit fighting against each other and unite against everyone else. The meeting lasted six hours. None of us involved remembers exactly what was said (or isn't sharing), but by the end, we were together. Paige: "I do remember feeling liberated in finally having a chance for everyone involved to say what was bothering them. I feel like we might even have started the meeting by saying that the point of the meeting was to be honest, open, and the end goal was to figure out how to do the best thing for the team even if it meant not doing what you felt was best for you as an individual. I think we all left the meeting knowing the team came first and we'd have to swallow our pride to make sure that was reality."

The team that emerged from the Carleton Chapel (where we'd met) wasn't the one that went in. Julia: "I think that coming out of the meeting I knew that our success would be a culmination of our skill, our determination, our belief (it was the first time in my life that I wholeheartedly bought into the idea that you could believe something into reality), and our joint effort as leaders to work together, keep the peace, and honor each individuals assets. Does that sound sentimental? My experience with Syzygy was very emotional. I think that the meeting was a turning point. It was a re-affirmation of our competitive/determined/difficult personalities and that we could use together to form a human wall."

Two weeks later in Boulder, Colorado we willed our way to Syzygy's only national title by out-toughing the toughest team of the 90s, UNCW.

DOUBLEWIDE

Clown Tent isn't limited to team chemistry; it can be an important piece of strategy and tactics. For many teams, it emerges by necessity; they build one set of rules for the team, but need their stars to do much more. Often, this creates a weird culture of confusion where the team is saying do one thing and yet the star players are doing something else. That isn't a failure of strategy; it is a failure of communication.

In the last two years, Doublewide of Texas has emerged as a national power largely due to their integration of Florida star Brodie Smith. They have done this by building an offensive system that most of their players follow, but allowing Brodie to do what he wants. Everyone else works around him. This is an offensive system philosophically similar to the Sockeye defensive scheme described in the first CT article; most players on the field are following a fairly strict set of rules, but one or two players are given near-total freedom.

The rules of Doublewide's system are simple. Run a standard vertical stack offense. Handlers and cutters know your roles and execute them. Brodie has priority on everyone else. As an example, take a look at a snippet from the Goat-DW quarterfinal from Nationals. (You'll want to start about 10:40 in.) Everyone gets in the vertical stack; Brodie has set up on the backhand sideline, effectively shutting that lane down for anyone else. The disc is swung back and forth. Comeback cuts happen. (But not on the backhand side because Brodie is clogging it.) Cutters and handlers work to provide options; Brodie does nothing. Finally, he goes into motion, first cutting all the way across the field, running through the middle of the stack before turning up and going deep. In the process, he breaks at least four rules of running a vertical stack offense. He also scores the goal, making a very difficult catch look routine.

Not convinced? Still think that Doublewide's system is unsuccessful because they haven't won a ring yet? Because they can't beat Revolver? Answer this trivia question: how many times did pre-Brodie Doublewide get farther than quarters?

16
WATCHING ULTIMATE IN THE VIDEO AGE

On watching ultimate video

Published January 11, 2012

I am swimming in video right now. USA Ultimate is releasing the footage from Club Nationals and friend-of-Fugue Luke Johnson sent me all the footage from Oregon's trip to Boulder last May. (You won't be getting the link to that one.) Video study is really a new thing in ultimate; prior to the digital age we live in today, the expense and difficulty of filming and producing meant that there was almost nothing to watch. Each year a single video of the Finals might come out, but it wasn't realistic for teams to film their own games on a regular basis – now it is standard practice. This newness means that we are all still learning how to go about watching videos. Here's what I've figured out, but I am also very interested in ideas that other folks have.

1. **WATCH WHOLE GAME FOOTAGE.** Highlights are awesome and cool and...awesome...and cool. They're not very useful. You can cut and paste a highlight reel together that makes one team look fantastic and the other terrible, regardless of the actual outcome. Beyond narrative fidelity though, you really need the whole game footage to understand what is going on. The plays where everything breaks down are just as important as the ones that go bang-bang-bang-goal.

2. **WATCH IT ONCE FOR NARRATIVE.** We are all human. We want to know what happens. We want to be wowed. We want to hear and see the story. It is very difficult to do any meaningful analysis while distracted by the story. I always begin by watching a video straight through without writing anything down. Just watch.

3. **CHART THE GAME.** This one is tricky, because what you choose to chart will go a long way toward determining your conclusions. Tross' (sorry, can't call him Mike) charting in his Ultimate Project videos is done at the possession level and segregates things out by long, medium and short. This choice of charting will then drive him to an analysis that focuses on field position and conversion rates, particularly on crucial short yardage situations. This is deliberate on Tross' part, because these are the things he is interested in as an analyst. Another example from the same game is Kyle Weisbrod's. His initial statistics are all based on an O-line, D-line divide. This is a good choice for an elite club team because their O- and D- function as separate units. It is a bad choice for women's, college or HS teams who aren't as clearly segregated. The piece I really like here is at the bottom: huck and reset comparisons. I like it because it is much more focused at the pass level. When I am charting, I prefer to go below the possession level and chart at the pass level. To do this, I take a team roster and chart each

pass. In the system I use, I don't break the passes down by type (yet), I am just counting them. When I am done, I have generated what is essentially a box score: passes, turns, goals and assists.

4. THE CHART IS THE BEGINNING. Once the charting is finished, I will look at it for anomalies or curiosities or patterns. Then I go back to the video and watch those plays in question. As an example, look at Kyle's chart from the DW-Truck game. Down at the bottom, Kyle breaks down the hucking percentage for each team. Truck went 1 for 10! As a coach for either team, I want to know why. Was it just poor execution? Was it something DW did defensively? Once I've identified the anomaly, I will go back and watch all the plays in question. (Kyle has obviously done this. His analysis is in the text above the stats.)

5. STRATEGIC PIECES. Not everything you want and need to see comes out of charting. Often, there is a piece or two that I remember from a game and I will watch film for that in particular. Last season, UNC Pleiades ran a zone that was causing us (Fugue) some trouble. I had footage from our game at Centex so I watched it frame by frame, each time drawing a field shot of the defense. The season before that, when we battled again and again with UW Element and really struggled to contain the Wilson-O'Malley connection, I spent a lot of time examining the structure of their resets to see if we couldn't get more pressure on that part of their game. (I know it might seem odd to look away from what was giving us trouble. The theory behind that idea is here.)

6. IMPLEMENTATION. The video work is really just the beginning. The next challenge is devising ways to implement the change that you have discovered you need, but that's a post for another day.

17

SIZE MATTERS: AUDL AND WOMEN'S ULTIMATE

On what a wider field does to the women's game

Published January 18, 2012

The birth of the AUDL brings with it three major changes: professionalism, refs and a wider field. Justifiably, most of the attention has gone to the first two of these. The impact of the wider field on playing style has been largely unmentioned, but I have some advice for the AUDL coaches: start watching women's ultimate.

There are many ways men's and women's ultimate differs, but at the strategic level they are different because the field is bigger in women's ultimate than in men's. While it is true that both men and women play on a 40×70, the differences in athleticism mean that the women's field is functionally larger. When explaining to men how women's and men's ultimate differed (especially new coaches), I would often ask them to imagine playing on a field that was 80 yards long and 50 yards wide. Currently, men's ultimate is really focused on a tight, vertical game that uses the spaces in front and behind the defender/cutter. With a wider field, women's ultimate is able to use much more lateral space to the sides of the defender/cutter. Without further ado, here are three strategic possibilities:

1. **TURN THE PAGE.** This is a classic cut at all levels of ultimate. Variously known as 'turning the page', 'the banana cut' or other more vulgar expressions, this move involves an out cut down one sideline and then a turn to the far back corner. The thrower fakes to the initial cut and then throws the giant outside-in across the field for the goal. This throw is practically forbidden in elite men's ultimate. The field is so narrow, the defenders so fast, the poaches so aware that the space to land that pass into is tiny. When I transitioned from Sockeye to coaching Syzygy, this throw drove me to fits. Jenn Willson would drop it in on other teams and I'd tell her: "You really shouldn't throw that." She'd look at me like "It worked." Over time, I gave up trying to stop her from throwing it because it worked! Only later did I realized that the reason it worked is because the field is bigger and the defenders' range smaller. The relative size of the field changed a bad throw (Sockeye) into a good one (Syzygy). The extra 13 yards of the AUDL field is more than enough extra room for this throw.

2. **ZONES WON'T WORK.** Actually, this isn't true. Despite the increased amount of space, zones obviously work at all levels of women's ultimate. The main reason is that the disc travels through the air quite slowly. A longer throw quite often has more hang on it and takes longer to travel than a snapped swing. To make the same distance in two passes is also quite slow because of the necessity to catch, pivot and release. Zones in the AUDL will need to modify their structure to account for the fact that there are more men who

can complete a 30 yard hammer consistently than women. A simple strategic adjustment like playing deeps left-right instead of up-back should solve that problem. There will be a lot of space to swing the disc, the trick will be to contain the play off of the swing.

3. NEW OFFENSIVE POSSIBILITIES. The challenge of designing an offense given new conditions is an exciting one. The current state of men's ultimate really only contains two choices: horizontal and vertical. I don't see a horizontal greatly improved by a wider field, but a vertical certainly is. There was a team called Godiva (you might have heard of them) who ran a ladder-continue style vertical stack offense that was quite effective. The difference between Godiva's and a team like Ironside's is timing versus cutting. Godiva's offense assumes the cut will be open if it can be timed right because there is lateral space to work into. Ironside's relies on the threat of the deep cut to free up the underneath. There is also an opportunity to run a new and more radically designed spread offense. Poaching has always been a major problem for the more innovative spreads and the width of field should make that more of a challenge for the defenders.

18
VISION

On team vision

Published February 8, 2012

It was with great enjoyment that I read Ben's excellent series last week. Since Ben and I can't talk about ultimate for 2 minutes without arguing, I have a million inconsequential disagreements but they really are inconsequential and not worth mentioning. There is however, a piece of getting great that Ben talked around but never addressed directly. As this piece is essential to how I coach, I'd like to address it; it is team vision.

The most important function of a coach is to create and articulate a team vision. What I strive to do is to build a picture in my head of what the team is going to look like on the field at Nationals. I don't mean the personnel or the uniforms, but the way the team is going to play. What is a point actually going to look like? How is our offense going to unfold? How will a defensive point play out? From here I start putting all the pieces into place of who will be where and doing what. This process will often go back and forth. It is impossible to build an initial vision without some sense of what you already have and how people fit into it. But every team is new every year (some are newer than others) and so the pieces will fit together differently and there will certainly be gaps that need filling.

Once you have that (always adjusting) picture in your head, take a good look at where you are. See what you have. See what is missing. Now comes the tricky part: you know where you are and you know where you want to be, but how do you get there? This is where a lot of the training and practicing methods Ben was discussing come into play. The role vision plays in this is to always guide you. As you think about strategy or tactics or drills or any aspect of the team's training regimen, consider your vision. Hold your vision in one hand and the work you are proposing in the other; does the work get you closer to where you want to be? Try another way. Compare where you are with where you want to be. What is the difference? What do you need to do to get there? Is your defense struggling around the disc? Design some drills to work on repositioning on handlers. Is your offense struggling to reach the deep cutters? Run some offensive simulations that physically move people in the way you have envisioned them moving.

This piece is equally true of players as well. The most helpful thing you can do as a coach is to see the player she will become and help her on her way. I know I am forever indebted to Eric Kehoe (Boston, Sockeye, current USAU observer) for looking at the young, rangy idiot from the Midwest who thought he was a receiver and seeing a handler.

I would have been okay as a receiver and that's the rub – okay. I'm still not sure what EK saw (I've never asked), but he was spot on. There is a bit of an art to seeing what someone can become, but the basis is paying attention and thinking about it. If you don't have a spot for someone or a sense of what they can become, that should bother you. I also am often looking (or seeing) for a flash or a spark more than consistent play. (Although consistency is a spark in its own right.) I am constantly reminded of a story I read once about single-A baseball tryouts. The scout was much more interested in the kid who from shallow left rifled the ball five rows up above first base while striving for the out than the weak-throwing but accurate short-stop. In that one play, with the ball clanging around in the empty seats, the scout saw possibility and potential. I don't necessarily agree that athleticism trumps skill and work ethic, but I do agree that it is the spark, the moment, the possibility that you are looking for.

I can't emphasize enough that these two pieces go hand-in-hand. You cannot build the possibility of your team without building the possibility of your players. As you progress toward your vision, the team and players will grow simultaneously. The work will narrow. In the beginning, changes will be quite large. Whole offensive or defensive structures will change. Cutters will become handlers, handlers will become cutters. As the season progresses and you get closer and closer to that vision, changes become smaller. A piece of the man offense needs tweaking. A handler needs work on breaking a backhand mark. The middle-middle in the zone needs to work on looking over his shoulder at the poppers more often. The challenge throughout is to choose the most beneficial work because there isn't time to do it all.

Here's the bad news. You won't ever get there. You'll get close. You'll reach your goal. You might even win the whole Big Thing. Getting to your vision is a lot like Zeno's Race Course Paradox; it keeps receding away even as it gets closer and closer. That's the brutality of teaching and coaching; even when you win you have to accept some failure.

19
THE THROWER'S EYE

On developing throws

Published February 15, 2012

Between the reality of technical skill and the black-and-white world of good and bad decisions lies an ocean of space. This space is defined by possibility; a possibility that is accessible if you can find it; a possibility where everyone is open all the time. To see this possibility you need the thrower's eye.

I remember my first moment of using the thrower's eye to throw someone open. It was 1993 and we (Carleton) had traveled to Ann Arbor for a club tournament in late April. It was a break-out year for the CUT and somehow we played our way into the semifinals against Night Train, the Michigan club team, who was coming off of a multi-year run at Club Nationals. We were still running 80s offense with its signature long, vertical stack and no dump, so all the resets came hooking off of the front of the stack. I was near the sideline, forced forehand into the middle of the field. The reset came down out of the stack and then J-ed away from me, toward the center of the field. Initially he was open, but the defender, reading the cut and the stall count, came flying down on the inside of the handler, completely flooding the throwing lane. It was a perfect opportunity for me to serve up the lay-out block. Instead, something strange and non-verbal and unthought happened. I rocked down into my pivot and threw a soft little blade that danced just out of reach of the charging defender before hooking back to wait for the handler.

What I threw was a forehand, but it wasn't a Forehand. The idea that there is only one Forehand and you have it or don't drastically over simplifies the situation. There are many, many, many forehands and which one you throw depends greatly on the situation. Also with this is the idea that there are Good Decisions and Bad Decisions. The question is more complicated that simply good or bad. Really, it is a question of choosing the right throw for the circumstance. Also, and I can't emphasize this enough, this isn't a thinking decision. You don't have time in a game to think and decide, you must simply see and throw. The challenge is what you see and training your eye to see. You must look beyond open or covered and see all kinds of things: the space, the match-up, the wind, the mark.

Finding that vision is a matter of experience and practice. You are trying to train your eye and body to read and react in an instant; to recognize and correct for a multitude of factors and then select from a multitude of options. When practicing, there are two pieces to work on: the technical and the vision. I separated the idea of the thrower's eye from the technical, but without actually having the skill, there isn't much you can do to take advantage of seeing the possibilities. How do you get the skill? You throw. Both Kung Fu Throwing and Wiggins' Zen Throwing routines are great places to start because they push you out of your initial comfort zone and into areas you haven't explored before. One piece that is in Wiggins' routine that is really important and can be greatly expanded on is visualizing while throwing. When you are working on a particular throw, especially a more esoteric one like a push or lefty backhand, the circumstances of use are pretty limited. (But like any specialized tool, the best tool for the job when the circumstances demand!) Hold these circumstances in your head while you are working. To use the lefty backhand as an example: when you throw it, you should feel the marker leaning in, the mistake of his arm too low, see the cutter flashing across in front of you, defender on his hip and the open space just out in front and upfield and then… throw it. You are training your eye to see and your body to react together. Without the visualization, you are only working the physical half of the equation.

The experience required to develop the thrower's eye comes through a huge number of repetitions and a huge amount of trial and error. There are three pretty good places to get these opportunities. The first and best is Mini. I can't say enough about Mini and its ability to help you improve your individual skills of marking, throwing, defending and winning. In a typical scrimmage of 7-on-7, even your top handlers are getting ~25 throws and your cutters far less. You'll get to 25 throws in 2 games of Mini. The statistics on marking and defending are similar. For our discussion, Mini provides a huge number of low-consequence repetitions to try out different throws and spaces. To maximize the effectiveness, prepare with the throwing visualization described above. The second best place is the summer fun tournament. Onion Fest (Walla-Walla) and Ho-Down (Calgary) were huge for my development as a thrower. I played them six or seven times apiece over my decade with Sockeye. That's almost 100 games to go out and play and experiment and create. Don't get me wrong; I played my ass off and played to win every time, but when I threw away a lefty-backhand trying to reach a 30-yard comeback cut, it wasn't a mistake of the same magnitude as a similar turnover while wearing a Sockeye jersey. The final opportunity to experiment is scrimmaging in practice. The consequences here are higher than the other two, but still not as high as in a real game. Think of practice as a dress rehearsal; it should look like just like a game, but if you flub, no one is watching.

The cutter is always open, if only you knew what to throw them.

20
KUNG FU THROWING

On practicing throws

Published February 22, 2012

I've been thinking a lot about KFT, both because throwing is a point of emphasis for Oregon this year, but also because of the Zen Throwing routine Wiggins recently published. What is interesting to me is how much each routine reflects the throwers who created it. You can see in KFT the rigor, precision and exacting repetition that makes Mike Caldwell so great. The piece of myself in KFT is pushing the boundaries of comfort, getting out to the margins and challenging what is possible. Wiggins' Zen Throwing fits him to a tee; it is control and focus.

Which system should you use? It really depends on you, both stylistically and the structure of your life. Start by trying each. You will need to do them twice before they make sense, because the first time through you are learning the What and not the How. One (or both) will resonate with you and that is the one you should use. You will also need to figure out how it will fit into your life. Mike and I created KFT when we were both husbands, new fathers, holding down full time jobs and playing Sockeye. A once a week workout that was 80 minutes door-to-door was essential to fit it into our lives. Right now, some of the Oregon women are using Ben's routine because they can do it in pieces by meeting up on campus between classes. 20 minutes here, 20 minutes there.

Enjoy!

Kung Fu throwing or Ninja throwing is a system developed by Mike Caldwell and I in 2005. I wanted to come up with a structured throwing plan to help developing throwers. As the only two Fish who lived on Capitol Hill at the time, Mike and I would meet often to throw. I solicited him to help me with this and to our surprise we found that it was an excellent system for established throwers. (We were in our 7th and 9th years on Sockeye.) We did KFT once a week the entire season and my throws were more consistently on than any other year.

The philosophy of the KFT seeks to improve a thrower in three ways. First and simplest, repetition. The entire program takes about an hour and features ~450 throws. Second, it seeks to challenge the limitations of a thrower by pushing them to throw beyond their comfort. Not so much in terms of distance, but in range of release. Lastly, the central portion of the program tries to articulate the different components of a throw. It separates the wrist from the arm from the shoulder from the hips from the feet. Young throwers are often limited to a single forehand where the handwristarmshouldertorsohipsfeet have to all be doing the same motion every time. What if a defender takes it away? What if you need to get around a marker? Really great throwers make adjustments large and small to their footwork and release points in order to beat defenders.

A warning about KFT: it is very physically rigorous. Mike and I felt taxed by it and we were in incredible shape and our bodies in ultimate Frisbee conditioning for years. KFT should be treated like a workout and you should pay attention to your body. Pay attention to the upper hamstring on your step leg (not your pivot leg) because that is where most of the stress of this workout goes. Also consider a partial workout to begin. Cut the 25s down to 15s or even 10s to start.

Here's the workout:

PART I – WARM UP W/ 25S

Throw 25 forehands, backhands and hammers at distances of 10, 20 and 30 yards

Throw 25 full lefty forehands, backhands and hammers at comfort distance (usually ~15 yards)

Stretch 5-10 minutes

Comments

Be disciplined about distance. The 10 yarder will feel way too short. You may not be able to throw hammers at the full 30. Try. When Mike and I developed it, my shoulders were wrecked and I couldn't throw a 30 yard hammer and so I just threw a mix of weird forehands and backhands. Throw the lefties. It is tempting to leave them out, but this workout really exacerbates the blacksmith syndrome inherent in training for ultimate and the lefty work will help balance you out.

PART II – THE KUNG FU

At comfort distance, throw 10 forehands and backhands…

As low as you can release

As far as you can release from your body

As high as you can release

Compass throwing. Imagine a compass with your pivot foot at the center. Pivot N and throw. Pivot NE and throw. Pivot E and throw and so on around the compass. Go four times around, twice throwing forehands and twice throwing backhands.

Rinky-dink. Throw 100 throws at a distance of 2-yards. The goal is rapid catch and release. Aim your throws to be easily catchable, but placed in such a way as to allow your partner to practice a variety of catches. Don't regrip! However you catch, you should throw. If pancake, throw hamburger. If you claw-catch over your head, upside-down backhand.

Optional Throw 10s at comfort outside in and inside out.

Comments:

Completion rates should drop in this section. Mike and I had a focus goal of no turnovers the entire workout, but we never counted this section. The point is to challenge your technical and physical limitations, not to be perfect. Your throws in this section should feel awkward. The optional piece is there if you want. It makes the entire workout a bit long, but it is a nice extra piece of work.

PART III – HUCKING

Huck for 10 minutes.

Comment:

Skip this part if you and your throwing partner are very unbalanced in power.

PART IV – PIVOTING AND FOCUS

25s with pivot at comfort

Comment:

Fake, pivot, throw. You are working on a snap fake and quick grip transition. Forehand to backhand should be one handed. Backhand to forehand should be a small off hand check. If you are working on a particular move, now is the time to practice it.

PART V – STRETCH AGAIN

Do it. All the recent press about in ineffectiveness of stretching has to do with the effects of stretching before working out. The science on stretching after is still solidly pro-stretching.

21
TEAM TALK

On developing a team language

Published February 29, 2012

Let me set the stage. It is power pools in Sarasota. Ironside is playing Doublewide to win the pool. The winner gets the gravy quarter-final against an exhausted 4-seed (eventually Madison) and the loser gets Revolver in the semis. At 2-2, Ironside's Seth Reinhardt (#2) gets a huge open field block on Brodie and two passes later, Russell Wallack (#33) hits CUT-alum Christian Foster (#20) for the 3-2 lead and the break. Celebration ensues! But wait. Right in the middle of all the jumping and yelling and high-fiving, there is Wallack engaged in a serious conversation with Jasper Hoitsma (#6) and Misha Sidorsky (#9). Why? What are they doing? Why aren't they celebrating?

Because they are working. Like all good club players, they understand that at that level, it is no longer about the big things like can you throw a forehand or how do you run a dump-swing handler set. Those things are taken care of and it is the little things: the small misunderstandings, a step here or a step there, squeezing a window shut just a bit, a break-throw not seen, that make all the difference. I don't know what Wallack, Hoitsma and Sidorsky are talking about. It might be the goal throw, but I doubt it – that was a no-brainer. It might be Wallack's reaction to the odd DW handler defense. It might be a piece of defense that happened 6, 8, 10 throws ago. The point isn't the particulars, it is the talking.

Like many things in ultimate, elite club players are much better at this kind of talk than college or high school players. They come equipped with a much better skill set; not a technical skill set, but an intellectual skill set. First, their experience is such that they can cut quickly through all the layers of unimportant stuff to get to the one or two important details. They have the intensive vocabulary necessary to have this conversation quickly. Most elite players have a history of team leadership as captains of their college teams and with that history comes a lot of talking about ultimate in casual conversation, team meetings, huddles and practices. Finally, most elite club teams are much flatter hierarchically than college or high school teams. The kind of conversation we are looking at is peer-to-peer, not captain-rookie or coach-player. They are working together to figure out a little problem.

How do you make this happen for your team? I have two big suggestions. First, vocabulary. You want to try to get everyone's frisbee vocabulary up to speed as quickly as possible. Personally, I prefer to do this through immersion. I just use jargon constantly and don't 'dumb-down' what I am talking about. Later, I may check in with rookies to make sure they got the ideas and knew all the words, but mostly I just go and assume it'll make sense. Second, you have to make room for people to disagree and be wrong. If as a coach or captain, you need it to always be your way and you are always butting into other people's conversations to 'correct' them, you may be getting what you want in that instance, but you are killing the kind of growth that is possible when the entire team is engaged mentally with the strategic and tactical problems. You can't oversee everything, so if you can get more and more of your team to be thinking and considering and talking, your team will be that much more powerful.

22
DRILL THEORY

On drills

Published April 19, 2012

I've been thinking about drills a lot recently. At Oregon, we are in the process this year of implementing a new offense, so there are all sorts of little problems to be sorted out. As the season progressed, we also felt more and more that our warm up didn't fit what we were trying to do and wasn't doing a very good job of preparing us. So there has been lots of new drills, some of which work and some of which don't. To cap all this off, three of the ex-Fuguers went down to try out for Fury last month. Among the many conversations we had about it, one of them commented: "It seems like someone, probably Matty, identifies a problem, comes up with a solution and a way to drill it and they drill the hell out of it." Here are some tips for you to develop and implement drills.

KEEP IT SIMPLE. Build up only when you've mastered a step. It is really tempting to make a drill "realistic" and try to account for all the what-ifs that come up. You can't and you will only muddy the purpose of the drill. As an example, take working on the dump-swing out of the trap. Imagine presenting this for the first time to your team (as will be the case with any new drill you invent). At first, this should be a 4 person drill with two people (marker and swing) just standing. The thrower faces the mark (who's standing), the A-handler fakes up line and cuts for the dump, dump is thrown, swing is thrown to the B-handler (who's standing). Once this has all been mastered, you add in the motion of the B-handler to work on timing. Then increase the defensive percentage of the marker to 50% or so. Are your starters hitting this 100% of the time and the team 90%? Add defenders on the handlers, again at 50% or so. Throughout, the process is practice-master-add. Be careful not to add to much. If you get up to five or more players, you aren't really running a drill anymore; you've crossed over into a scripted scrimmage, which is a different animal.

DON'T GAME THE DRILL. Always remember the purpose of the drill and be disciplined about performing your roles, particularly defenders in an offensive drill and offenders in a defensive drill. People hate to lose and often feel that if they are shut down or beat, they have lost. If you are running a drill to work on fronting comeback cuts, don't let the cutters go out. If you are working on dump-swing, don't let the marker take away the dump entirely.

DON'T WORRY ABOUT ROTATION. When you introduce a new drill, don't try to figure out or teach the rotation. In fact, don't worry about it at all. Just tell people to make sure they move through the drill and get to all the spots. The rotation will develop naturally and more quickly than if you have to try to teach it.

MAKE SMALL ADJUSTMENTS. You want to resist the temptation to spend a lot of time talking about the drill (see below). The purpose of a drill is to teach muscle and image memory and words are the enemy of this. As captain or coach, you will have to stop the drill every now and again to make an adjustment, but it should only be for 30 seconds or so – one small idea, no more.

DO DRILLS OFTEN, BUT NOT FOR VERY LONG. When I was a young coach at Carleton, I did a lot of reading about the Jordan-era Bulls and Phil Jackson. One of the things I got to see was a practice schedule and I was struck by the fact that none of their drills took longer than eight minutes! I took two things away from that: they already knew all the drills and they used the same ones again and again. When I became a teacher, this theory of learning was confirmed: the best learning comes from a task that is repeated often for a short period of time.

WORKING GROUP. When Fugue was working on developing a new warm up, Shannon McDowell came up with all the possible new drills and then one day after practice we ran through them with a mixed group of 8 players, captains and coaches. This allowed us to run through them, stop and talk about difficulties and make adjustments so that when we introduced them to the team at the next practice the major problems where already ironed out.

Good luck!

23
ONLY ONCE
On being a part of a team

Published April 25, 2012

I have been on five teams in my career: Carleton-B, CUT, Syzygy, Sockeye and Fugue, but a more honest count is 24 teams. Each season, each team is different. Certainly there are similarities year to year, but the character of the team is different every year. Teammates change, expectations change, who you play and where you play and how your team performs; all these things are different and so the identity of the team is never the same. All of this means that the team you are on right now, the team that is coming closer and closer to the end of its season, will exist only this once.

One of the great delights of ultimate is getting to know my team each year. You'd think that Sockeye 2005 would have been the same team as Sockeye 2004, but they stood on opposite sides of a gulf: one team had a ring and the other didn't. You'd think that CUT 1994 and 1995 would be the same: 13 of 18 players returned, but those two teams couldn't have been more different. Even when seasons are tough and the personality of a team not what you had hoped (yes, a few of those 24 years were unhappy ones) there is a satisfaction in coming to understand something.

I'm not going to give you Fugue 2012. The joys and frustrations, successes and failures, all the hard work and growth; these things are ours and you have yours. Your team is like someone you love that you only get to be with for a little while and then they're gone. You won't really know them until the very end of the season. Endings are so critical to what we do that the character of the team won't necessarily reveal itself until the very, very end. So when you go out to practice this week, when you hit the fields at Regionals this weekend or the next, savor and cherish the moment: you won't get it again.

24 THROW YOUR FIRE

On throwing your fire

Published May 9, 2012

...before it's too late. Seriously.

I know I really should be talking about seeding at Nationals or how Fugue is preparing or who I think is going to win Open or how to game plan for Boulder, but instead I want to help you with something much more important. All you impulsive people probably don't need to read this because you've already thrown yours and all you cautious people will likely just ignore what I have to say, but if I can convince just one cautious ultimate player to throw their Fire I'll have made the world a better place.

Don't even start with that: "I'm saving it for something important" business. You only get the one Fire, so whenever you choose to throw it, it is a Once In A Lifetime Experience. By definition, whatever you throw your Fire on is important just because you used your Fire on it. The other reason to throw it soon is that it has more value now than it will in ten or fifteen or twenty years. As soon as you retire from ultimate, your Fire depreciates exponentially. If you have the bad luck to marry a non-frisbee player your Fire instantly has zero value. The person who hit the timing on this one the best has to be non-frisbee playing Carleton alum Chad Boger. He threw his to make an irritating, egotistical alumni bow down to him. How much worth would his Fire have now that he is a Minneapolis dentist?

25
US NATIONAL TEAM

On the composition of the US National team

Published August 1, 2012

With true Worlds in the books, it is time to start thinking about 2016's campaign, a surprisingly short four years away. The time has come to put away the winner-goes system and implement a true National team.

Like 2004 and 2008, USA came away with gold and silver in the main two divisions. There was a swap this year as the men took care of business, while the women faltered. Even in victory, the Team USA men looked shaky in struggling with Australia and Canada. Comparing results from true Worlds and club Worlds shows an even more startling result. USA has won every gold medal (except in 2006, when the distance to Perth kept all but a partial Subzero away.) When the talent pool is level, no one can challenge the US. When other nations are combine their talent to make a super team, suddenly things are much more even. Team Japan won women's this year by combining the top players from UNO, Huck and MUD. There is no question that a US National Team would out talent every other team in the world.

The challenge for any club team in a Worlds year is the double peak. You play a spring season built to peak at Worlds and then a fall season to peak for club Nationals in Sarasota. This double peak is extremely difficult to manage both physically and mentally. In 2008, Sockeye and Fury attempted an audacious triple: win the Dream Cup, win true Worlds, win Club Nationals. Fury pulled it off, but Sockeye missed on all three by a combined 5 points. When I watched both Revolver and Fury play in Sakai this July, I saw two teams that were incomplete. This was mostly evident on offense where both teams struggled with their conversion rate (goals/possessions). This number should be above 60% for men and 50% for women and in none of their big games did they approach these numbers. I attribute this entirely to the double peak. When I have watched the Club Series versions of these teams, their hallmark has been a nasty ability to possess the disc regardless of what the other team was doing defensively. All the other teams at Worlds existed only for Worlds and their focus was only on Worlds, giving their efforts and focus a sharpness that will always be lacking from a team attempting a double peak. A US National team would be built for Worlds and its focus would be right there.

The obvious rebuttal to this argument is that team chemistry outweighs talent every time. The immediate and snarky reply is "have you watched any NexGen in the past week?" Chemistry is an issue and deserves a more serious reply than that. Preparation has to be taken very seriously; the process and planning around a National team should be longer and more extensive than the current infrastructure around the U-19 and U-23 teams. The U-19 girls lost in 2010 to Colombia in part because they'd never been in a close game before that one; they had the talent to win, but not the experience together as a team. Fortunately, the summer before true World is open on the WFDF worlds rotation, opening the possibility for a two year preparatory campaign. Chemistry is a concern, but it is a beatable concern.

The final piece in my argument has not to do with competition, but fairness. In the history of Worlds, if you haven't had the luck to play for a team from Seattle, San Francisco, NY or Boston you were never going to have the chance to represent your country at worlds. It doesn't matter how good you were, you weren't going to get to go. World Games has remedied this to an extent, but only 10 players actually make the trip: 6 men and 4 women – not exactly a full sampling of talent.

The standard for US Ultimate is gold and a National team will get us there consistently.

LATE ADDENDUM:

USA Ultimate responded to a my request for comment on the US National team with the following statement:

"Refining our selection processes to sustain international excellence for all of our national teams is a significant component to our new strategic plan, which was revealed during the opening session at the U.S. Open convention earlier this month.

Although we won't be rolling out the entire plan in detail until later this fall, now would be a great time to discuss our strategy, specifically as it relates to international competition while it's on the front burner with WUGC and WJUC all current. "

26
IT'S THAT SIMPLE

On some easy tips to winning

Published October 11, 2012

Watching NW Regionals a week ago, I was struck by a small and simple thing that separates the great teams from all the rest: they threw to open people. More importantly, they never looked off open people, which is what I saw a lot of other teams do. And while it is that simple, there are some hidden elements to making it happen for your team.

The great teams are functioning with purpose and clarity. Their throwers and receivers are on the same page to know what cut should happen under what circumstances. The thrower looks for it and the cutter provides it. Additionally, great players are really good at knowing what their teammates are capable of and factoring that into their cutting. A typical situation will offer several cutting options and smart players choose the one that they know the thrower can hit. *Lesson: know your team's plan and know your teammates.*

There is an obvious technical element to this. The great teams are loaded with great throwers who can seemingly hit cutters everywhere on the field. Hucking gets a lot of attention, but it isn't as difficult a skill as breaking the mark. While superstars' ability to throw gets a lot of attention, it is one that almost anyone can attain with work. When you watch someone throwing amazing throws, you are watching someone who has invested a lot of time getting better. The resources are out there (Kung Fu, Zen, disc golf) but the simplest thing is to put on the cleats and throw every day. *Lesson: If you want to be great, you've got to put in the time with the disc. Throw.*

The last piece is the simplest and the most difficult. When someone is open, you have to throw it to them. We make barriers in our minds (particularly about break throws) that keep us from throwing to open people. If it is a short throw and the cutter has a step of separation, you have to throw it. Period. It doesn't matter what the marker is doing, you have to hit that cutter. Looking people off because you don't trust them or they're on the break side or you want something better leads to the slow constricted death of your offense. *Lesson: When your teammate has separation, throw it to them.*

27
THE MONKEY ON OUR BACKS

On SOTG

Published October 17, 2012

I watched the giant firestorm that erupted in the aftermath of the Team Japan – Team Canada game at Worlds this past summer and felt like it was actually good for the health of Spirit of the Game. SotG is dependent on the relationships between players, teams and community. Here was an example of a team making mistakes (which happens) and the community holding them accountable for it. Even more impressive, Furious issued an apology and worked to change some of the problematic elements of their game.

I had a chance to catch up with Morgan Hibbert and Mark Seraglia at NW Regionals. It was immediately clear from that conversation that Furious (like all teams) is divided internally about how SotG should be managed and this situation in particular. Both Morgan and Seraglia were completely willing to own up to their mistakes in that game. Hibbert said, "We felt that the Japanese were cheating us, so we had to have a temper tantrum. It was dumb and I immediately snapped out and was glad I hadn't hurt that guy [after backpacking him]." (Italics added.) Within their contrition was a blasé been-there-done-that approach to their mistakes that many, many club players carry. When you play as long as these guys have, you are going to screw up sometimes and you have to find a way to live with it. This blasé attitude is why club SotG is better than college SotG; no one gets too worked up because they've seen it all before. It is clear that not everyone on the team feels this way. When I asked Morgan and Seraglia about the apology Furious issued in response to the situation, they said it "was something the media and outreach guys thought we needed to do, so they just did it" without consulting with the team as a whole.

Furious had actually begun making changes to their approach to SotG prior to Worlds. The biggest change they were trying to make was to contain the "yapping from the sidelines" and the us-against-the-world mentality that had propelled Furious for so many years. The main impetus for the change was not the Canada-Japan game, but the ongoing transformation of Furious following the Lugsdin-Grant-Cruikshank years. All during that period, Furious would use an opponent's call or reaction to get their sidelines and teams riled up and emotionally driven. This would bring a two-part jab: a huge hate-dump on their opponent and greatly increased intensity on defense. (During those years, part of my job with Sockeye was to act as a lightning rod to absorb the hate-dump and shield the rest of the team.) Furious was moving away from this strategy because it was no longer "was helping the team." As the team personnel transformed due to retirement and recruitment, what had been effective now was detrimental and a change was needed.

I wonder about the long-term impact on SotG and Furious. For SotG, it is a benefit. After we get over the knee-jerk reaction of "Spirit is broken, we need refs" the long term impact will be proof that the community as a whole can help teams and individuals do what is right. Peer pressure matters. Think it doesn't? The dirty looks, people turning away from you in conversations, the nasty little remarks.... these things add up. It is no surprise that periodically individual teams develop really bad SotG – their internal and community peer pressure is broken. There were some aspects of this incident that really trouble me. The attacks on Team Canada were very nasty and very personal. Both Morgan and Seraglia recieved multiple personal emails attacking them and their actions in that game. To me, that crosses a line.

For Furious, they are still a team in transition. This transition is happening both with their play and with their internal psyche. Like any team in transition, they can play incredibly inconsistently, as was witnessed at NW Regionals when they played terribly on Saturday and then redeemed their weekend by crushing Voodoo and edging Rhino on Sunday, but even that was tinged by controversy. As Seraglia said at the end of the interview, "We're the same cheaters we've always been. And mention my shit-eating grin."

Clarification: In the rush at the end of our interview (the Rhino game was starting) I had misconstrued the sequence of events that led to the apology to Team Japan. I had a chance to speak with Morgan Hibbert via email today. He clarified the situation, "Initially we decided we weren't going to respond but after some time Alex Davis approached me about wanting to write something. After him and I conferred I then made the final call that we would write something."

28
MEASURING POSSESSION

On metrics for possession in ultimate

Published November 14, 2012

'Possession' gets thrown around a lot without a clear understanding of what it means from an analytical standpoint. A big part of the issue is one of vocabulary; we generally lack good terminology to describe the various attributes of possession. One way to facilitate thinking is to pull a concept apart, breaking it into more well-defined pieces. Because the discussion and thinking around possession is still evolving, the names for these pieces are drifting. These are the ones I use; you may have heard something different.

EFFICIENCY (= GOALS SCORED/POSSESSIONS)

This is the most useful of stats for predicting victory. Because ultimate is an alternating possessions game and each point is only worth one, the team that is more efficient wins. Period. By definition, that crazy-throwing karma team is more efficient than the steady dump-swing team, if they win. Efficiency is a really useful stat for setting team goals. It is also a really helpful way to think about possession above the pass level. Steve Moons was the first person I heard really articulate the idea of a "win-line" – the efficiency percentage you must reach to win. For Club ultimate in the 90s, Steve put the win-line at 60%. If you were more efficient than that, you'd almost always win. In the last decade or so, it may have crept upwards slightly, but only slightly. For reference, I'd put college men's and women's club at 50% and college women's at 40%.

RETENTION (= PASSES COMPLETED/PASSES ATTEMPTED)

What is nice about retention is that you can really focus in on an individual's performance. If you have the luxury of filming every game and the time to digest all that film, over the course of a season you can get a really good statistical look at how individual players are performing. Like all statistics, don't read too much into a single game; there just isn't enough data. If you want to look at a single game, you are much better treating it as a case study than as statistics. A final note: a retention number below 90% is abysmal.

The biggest danger of retention is that you confuse it with efficiency. The goal of ultimate is not to complete passes, but to score goals. Completing passes is a necessary but dangerous requirement to score goals. All too often, teams focus on completion instead of conversion. Claiming they are a 'possession' team, they are frustrated in losing to a team that is a lot less 'disciplined.'

The calculation of this statistic is a little tricky on the ends. How do you count a dropped pull or a dropped goal? The clearest way I have seen is to count an individual's 'pass attempt' as being with a catch and ending with a successful throw. The goal catch becomes a 'pass attempt' with no pass but counts for that person's retention.

CONVERSION (= GOALS SCORED/POINTS PLAYED)

In a way, this statistic is almost meaningless because it is right there to see in the final score of any game. It does have its uses though, particularly if you are playing O-line and D-line. It allows you to segregate the data into those two groups and take a look at how each has performed. Club teams typically shoot for a 70+% O-line conversion and a 30+% D-line conversion rate. (As long as your O-line + D-line conversion totals more than 100%, you win.) This sets up a wonderful staple of club team practice – the 10 pull. Defense pulls ten times, not trying to win, but just beat their conversion goal. Only 2 D goals? Offense wins. Four or more D goals? The defense. Finishing the scrimmage 7-3 is a push.

Another area conversion is helpful is in terms of overall team strategy. For a possession oriented team (like DoG or Revolver) focusing on efficiency is a really useful goal. However, for a less possession oriented team (like Doublewide) it is often smarter to focus on conversion. Taking chances the way they do, they know they are likely to turn it over. The focus no longer is solely on possession, but a more holistic approach to scoring that emphasizes defense and smart risk taking.

29

SARASOTA MORNING

On poetic starts to nationals

Published October 24, 2012

I wake up before everyone and slip out of the hotel into the dark. As I walk toward the beach under the glow of the street lamps, the Palm Bay is absolutely silent. Tonight, when all but two are done, this road will be alive and screaming with drunk frisbee players finally free to cut loose after their months of abnegation. But right now, it's silent. The Gulf water is surprisingly cool. I swim back and forth parallel to the beach and my body starts to open up and let go. Every year this gets harder and harder and it takes more and more work just to be ready to warm up. I try to think about this and not think about sharks. I think about sharks.

Now I'm in the back seat of the car, listening to this year's music. I like this year's music, which is a good thing because we'd listen to it even if I didn't, just because that's what you do. But I like it, so I sing quietly to myself. Clark is empty this morning and the expanse of it is staggering. You could easily fit a field crossways to the road between the strip mall on the left and the strip mall on the right. Thursday's and Friday's commuters are still abed and we fly down this asphalt prairie toward I-75. We see carloads of other players; there's Ozone and there's some Madison guys and the DC guys. We wave to Ozone, but there's too much on the line now with the other Open teams, so unlike the friendliness of the early days, we studiously ignore each other.

The field is buried in mist when we get there and we pile out quietly. Our tracks linger in the grass, crossing this way and that, each leading invisibly to its own field and pair of teams. These misty mornings are one of my very favorite things about Nationals and I am glad today is one of them. I greet my teammates as they filter in. Just a word and a touch; we know what is coming. We've stumbled and now we sit here getting ready for quarterfinals against another juggernaut. Semifinals is the distinction that separates contenders from the rest and while there would be disappointment in losing at that stage, there is no shame. Losing in quarters will be shameful. I know the team we are playing; they feel the same way. One of us will be done in a few hours.

We begin the warm up with my body and my mind on autopilot. I know my body will get warm. I know I will be focused. The ritual will take care of that. Trusting in the preparation, I pull a bit of myself back and away to do damage assessment. The aching ribs, the whiplash and the hotness in my wrist can all be ignored. They are just the price of playing defense and in a way I welcome them as signs of a job well done. I'm worried about my ankles, but they feel alright, so I put them aside and focus on the real problem. There's a little burr in my hamstring that won't disappear and won't let go. It's small, but it's not firing at all. So my warm up becomes a process of finding out what I can and can't do; how I will work around this unusable piece of muscle. There's a real risk of serious injury, so if this were any other day I wouldn't play. It isn't any other day. All through this personal work I am checking in with the other defenders. I take the measure of yesterday's injuries. We're banged up, but everyone is going to play. Good. I spend a minute talking with a teammate who is struggling and try to assess his mental state. Hard to tell. We'll have to wait and see if he can play his way out. My throws are ready. They're not great, so this won't be a wondrous day with the disc, but they're enough on that I'm not going to turn it over.

Sometime during our preparations, the sun came out and burned off the mist. We never really dried out, though, we just transitioned from damp to sweaty without noticing. Some of my teammates are changing into dry socks and some are having a last minute snack. Some of the defenders take a moment to talk over match-ups, but there's not much to say. We've already gone over this last night. Into the final huddle. The captains say the things I knew they were going to say. We cheer. We are starting on offense, but that's no big deal. They'll score and I'll play. Here we go.

30
POACHING ON THE VERT

On poaching d

Published July 17, 2013

I watched the Sockeye-NexGen game last night with increasing frustration as Sockeye's very vanilla defense completely failed to generate any defensive pressure. I don't blame Sockeye; it is the smart strategic play for a team that depends on poaching, switching and playing mysterious defenses to try to keep them off of video on demand. So while some of my aggravation was watching the Fish get run over, most of the aggravation was watching vert-stack offense run unimpeded. Fifteen years ago, vert-stack offenses were grinding to a halt as anti-vert defensive know-how permeated the upper echelons of the sport. En masse, the entire sport switched over to running ho-stack. Now that vert is new again, that defensive wisdom is missing.

The system described below isn't the only way to throw a wrench in the works, so take it with a grain of salt. Any system you use has to work for your team and your personnel. This is meant to be a starting place and a thinking point more than a proscriptive system.

This is a three-man switch. The players are an On-Man defender, the Poacher and the Cleaner. Everyone else can play regular stare-at-your-guy defense, but they need to keep their ears open. To illustrate how this might develop, I'll describe a classic lane cutting situation, typically a comeback cut, although this will work for an out-cut as well. The On-Man is on the primary cutter and clearly defines what he is covering (for the purpose of this example, he covers the out). The Poacher comes out of the stack to cover the under. Three men are in the lane now, two defenders and the cutter. So far, this is absolutely routine. The lane cut should be dead, but there are now two loose offensive players somewhere on the weak side.

The Cleaner's job is to get everyone reassigned and playing man-on again as quickly as possible. He can cover one of the loose players himself and direct the Poacher on how to recover or he can direct the On-Man defender or the Poacher or any of the other defenders on where to go and how to switch. (Technique: yell the name of the defender and point where you want them to go. They go.) The reason this is vague is because there are so many different scenarios depending on the circumstances: thrower, wind, other player-pairs, etc, etc. It is the Cleaner's job to see through this jumbled situation and get everyone reassigned.

This system works best when you have three heads-up, sophisticated defenders on the field. That gives you a high likelihood of having them where they are in good position to poach/switch (out of the middle of the stack) and in a spot where they can direct traffic as the Cleaner. Tactically, you want your help defenders on the other team's lesser players and your on-man defenders on their main-cutters.

The essential skill you need from all your players is awareness. The switches and the responsiveness to the Cleaner can't happen if they are overly fixated on their assignment. Poachers need a certain degree of recklessness and a nose for the block. A Cleaner needs the ability to instantly analyze the situation and make a judgement. (Can you close your eyes and point to all thirteen other players on the field? And explain what they are doing?)

So how do you get your team here? Free your best defenders to experiment and make mistakes. When a rookie botches their footwork and gets beat on the open side, you don't blame the system – you help them learn and adjust. If your team doesn't have a system for poaching and switching, then even your best players are like rookies. The challenge is to suffer through the short term failures as your prepare for long term success. A committed coach helps this process, but you can get there without one, it'll just take more conversation among the team leadership. As your defenders grow, they will develop their own system and personality – it might look like this one, it might be completely unique.

31
NATIONAL CHARACTER

On what the world's all about

Published August 14, 2013

I'm sorry I've been gone, there are some big changes coming to *Win the Fields* (see below) that needed sorting out. In the meantime, I'll have some odds and ends for the next few weeks.

It was awesome to get to watch the U-23 and World Games; the viewing highlight might have been running the NexGen and IamUltimate streams on simultaneous split screens. I was struck by how similarly National teams played across different divisions; Team Japan looked like Team Japan whether it was U23 Mixed or World Games. Ditto for Canada, the US, Colombia…

Below is my assessment of national character and a rating for each of the six World Games nations.

USA

The Americans are the most vanilla of teams, relying on superior talent and superior depth. There isn't much sneaky or surprising or even weird about what the Americans are doing; they're just playing basic ultimate better than everyone else.

Rating: A. They've chosen a strategy that fits their personnel. There's no need to be tricky if you've got the horses.

CANADA

Priority number one is mean, nasty (mostly man-to-man) defense from every player. Offensively, the plan is to get the foot soldiers out of the way of stars and let them work. Big spaces and big throws.

Rating: B. This is a great strategy for making a lot of mileage out of a small talent pool. Canada's current difficulties are that their current stars are not up to the stature of Lugsdin, Grant, Cruikshank and Calder. Still, their execution is excellent.

JAPAN

The Hayate has come to (intentionally) characterize Japanese ultimate. Lots and lots of short, quick throws into crowded spaces. Defensively, lots of sagging and help defense, particularly around the disc. This defense doesn't generate much pressure, but it does challenge the opposition to be patient and technically sound.

Rating: B-. There are too many passes that don't generate easy progress. Their defensive strategy isn't great at creating blocks. For a team whose express goal is winning gold, they will likely have to climb down off of this particular hill in order to get to the top of the mountain.

COLOMBIA

Creative and athletic. Colombia has a lot of success throwing the things you think they won't. They are rapidly gaining in sophistication, too. Their World Games work showed a growth and maturity that had been lacking in their previous work.

Rating: B+. The challenge moving forward will be to harness their creativity – to trim the unproductive aspects of it without losing the brilliance.

AUSTRALIA

Hard running and versatile. It is tricky to key in on any one aspect of their game because everyone does everything. They throw more mid-range (20-30 yard) passes than anyone else.

Rating: B+. They are cohesive and use their personnel well. A tighter plan in endzone offense would make a big difference.

Special note: Tom Rogacki is Top 5 all time. If he'd played in North America, we'd all know his name.

GREAT BRITAIN

A bit one dimensional – huck it to the big guys. It works because they've got some excellent big guys, but it isn't high enough percentage or sophisticated enough to beat the top teams.

Rating: C. The limits of this strategy were brutally revealed in Cali. The problem with being a one-trick pony is that some games need a different trick.

32
PRESSURE

On switching tides

Published August 21, 2013

I spent last weekend cooking and watching the West Coast Cup. It's hard to express how delightful it is to have live ultimate to watch from home. The tournament got me thinking about all sorts of things, but I was most struck by the similarity of three games: Sockeye v. Revolver, Rhino v. Bravo and Rhino v. Sockeye. In each of these games, the underdog took a lead into half and then blew it. This situation is classic in ultimate; I'd be hard-pressed to count how many times I've seen a younger/more inexperienced/less talented team take a halftime lead only to cough it up in the second half. It's the pressure.

The pressure comes from two different sources, one real and the other imagined, but both equally powerful. Great teams have the ability to raise their level of play when circumstances require it. Often, the underdog takes their lead because the favorite isn't playing their best. Then, after half or a "stop sucking!" huddle, the favorite raises their level of play, usually through increased defensive intensity, break follows break and…the game is over. The second type of pressure is the pressure of circumstance, the realization that "we're beating so-and-so!" and the weight of actually winning, of actually making plays, starts to wear on a team. The last thing you possibly want to do while you are playing is to think about the implications of what you are doing. (In fact, you don't want to be thinking at all.) Often, it is a combination of the two, the real and the imagined, that dooms a team.

The two Rhino games are classic examples of this phenomenon. Of particular note is Rhino's body language during Sockeye's run early in the second half; they are feeling the weight of the situation. The Sockeye game is notable in that they are able to fight off the pressure and pull out the win – it is a quite remarkable piece of work. First, Revolver brings the heat – their defense to start the second half is excellent and their offense in transition focused and precise. Mentally, the Fish must feel the weight of their recent years' frustrations against Revolver. Then, after they'd given up the lead, something amazing happened. They steadied themselves and reversed the pressure. They began converting on offense and creating opportunities on D. BJ Sefton made a huge play and tipped the scales and the Fish hung on to win.

Looking at the three games gives some insight into how this type of game happens and how you can win it if you are the underdog. First, you have to both accept and ignore the situation. If you are on a team that is struggling to win close games, you are going to think about all those games you've lost. If you always lose to some team, you will think about those losses when you play that team. You can't help it. But what you can help is how you respond. The trick is to accept the circumstance, including that you are in your own head about it, and just start fighting. Defense is the best way because it is brain-on-fire. Fight and struggle and fight some more and let that be your attitude and your message in the huddle. Focusing on defense allows you to actually go on the offensive and claim back the initiative in the game. (It is a peculiarity of ultimate that defense is aggressive and offense passive.) One of the ways underdogs lose these games is that they lose initiative and control – defense will help get that back. The final advantage focusing on defense has is that it keeps you from focusing on turnovers. Focusing on turnovers is brutal when you are giving up a lead, because it puts your team's energy on the very thing that is burying you instead of on the thing that will lead you out.

The last two pieces might be the most important. If you are in a catch-up/underdog situation, the only long term solution is to work your ass off. It is hard work and the willingness to keep chopping that will eventually turn things around. Ask DoG. Ask the Condors. Ask Furious. Ask Sockeye. Ask Revolver. Finally, you've got to enjoy those games while you're in them. Embrace the challenge and go forward.

33
OMNIVOURE

On pulling ideas from everywhere

Published August 28, 2013

In this day and age of ubiquitous video, access to footage is easy and it is entirely possible to spend days and days watching film. Film has its uses, particularly analysis of yourself and other teams, but it isn't necessarily a great tool for new and creative thought. For that you need outside inspiration. I've always been an omnivore, pulling ideas from any and everywhere. Here are three examples:

OFFENSE: ASA MERCER V WASHINGTON

About ten years ago, Spring Reign, the Seattle middle school tournament, invited a bunch of Sockeye and Riot players out to come, hang out, play a showcase game and generally provide some prestige to the event. It was fun. The finals featured Asa Mercer and Washington middle schools. It was a good game. Mercer was lead by a rugged defender, who by poaching on Washington's deep shots was able to keep her team hang around. Unfortunately, Mercer didn't have the offensive chops to keep up as Washington literally ran away with it.

Washington was led by two tiny handlers who used a unique space and cutting style. (Remember that this was ~2001 during the heyday of the vert.) They took their five downfield players and spread them out all around the field, but were careful to keep the area in front of the disc clear. The two handlers then ran a wide open attacking set that gained huge yards for advantage. After catching the big runners their work had created, they'd pick out their shots to the downfield players who were open by the dramatic repositioning of the disc. This offensive concept – spread everyone out, create attacking motion with your handlers and then take shots downfield – became the foundation of Oregon's 2010 national championship offense.

DEFENSE: GRANTLAND

I've always loved this blog – it is far more analytic than most and therefore most interesting. I won't go into too great of summarizing detail because you can (and should) read the article. I saw two really great implications to take out of it. First and tangentially, is the futility of statistics in ultimate. Statistics are dependent on a large sample size, both in prediction and application. Another way to look at it is that you need a lot of data to say anything meaningful and you can only predict across a large number of events – a single event is just gambling. So until we get SportsVU in ultimate (wow!) a lot of statistics is guess work and horribly prone to confirmation bias.

There is also a defensive takeaway in here as well: help more. Defenders spend far too much time and effort covering people who aren't doing anything. Yes, 'just-guard-your-guy defense creates clarity. Yes, it helps your team build a 'man-up' attitude. Yes, it fosters accountability for your defenders. But it is rarely the most efficient thing to do. Go back and look at the film of the Japanese women from WUGC 2012 (here's pool play vs. USA) – that's the textbook film on using help to constrict space. There is a great deal of defensive growth to be made by adopting a basketball mentality of help and rotation.

LEADERSHIP: THE TYRANNY OF STRUCTURELESS

The lack of resources in ultimate force us into all sorts of weird leadership structures. Although most teams have settled into the now-standard captains plus committees system, I am constantly looking for was to improve leadership structure and to ensure the sustainability of it. (College teams in particular are prone to collapse with the graduation of institutional knowledge.) This article really does a great job of laying out the issues around building leadership structures and the possible solutions. I also stretched to consider whether the kind of issues discussed here extended onto the field – that is, if you use a structureless system of offense or defense are you just creating informal playing structures and making it that much harder for the uninitiated to figure out? As a bonus, for those of us interested in feminism and radical politics, the middle portion offers a window into the early development of the women's rights movement.

34
PLAYER COACHES AND COACHING COACHES

On coaching and establishing a team

Published September 4, 2013

Hi Lou,

There is a lot of advice out there, whether in the digital or physical world, that players can use to get better. However, as a coach, it is much more difficult for me to find resources on how to better coach Ultimate. Are coaches just tight-lipped when it comes to coaching, or is it more that most teams are so different in personality that a different coaching style is needed for each one? Or is it something completely different?

You're an experienced and successful coach, and rather importantly, willing to write about many things related to ultimate. Do you have advice on becoming a better coach? Is it directly related to being a better player?

I think that a lot of (young college) teams are looking to their captains to coach, and from running practices to devising strategy in games, the captain(s) often shoulder a heavy burden. Is it possible to be a 'good' player coach? Would it benefit the team to rope in a separate, non-player coach even if they were less knowledgeable about the game?

Thanks,
DG

DG,

While the kind of coaching resources you describe are largely missing from ultimate, there are lots and lots of great books and videos from other sports. As an example, the Inner Game of Tennis has had a profound influence on my coaching. Still, providing the kind of coaching resource you describe is a big part of why I write. Now to your question:

It is possible to be a good player-coach; that was the model for ultimate from its birth through the late 90s and beyond. Even now, the elite men's club teams are just beginning to get coaches. That said, there is a huge competitive advantage to having a non-playing coach. The challenge is to allocate responsibilities in such a way as to maximize everyone's strengths. If your non-playing coach isn't a great strategist, that doesn't mean they can't be a great help to a team by handling logistics, managing the clock at practice, calling subs and other non-analytical tasks. The key is for the entire leadership group to have good discussions about who is going to do what and to define

clear roles.

~

Hi Lou,

Last year I transferred schools and went from a large, established ultimate program to one where they played hotbox barefoot twice a week. By January, I was coach and we were running serious practices. By May the whole team had made serious improvements (in the strategy, fitness, and shoe departments). Between my previous experience and the huge amount of ultimate-related info on the web, I've been able to teach this group how to play better.

This next year is my last at this school and I've been trying to figure out how to create a self-sustaining ultimate program beyond my tenure. Do you have any advice on laying the foundation for a program?

Thanks!
Dave

Dave,

You have been teaching people how to play ultimate; this coming spring you will want to teach them how to be leaders. The biggest loss college teams face with the graduation of a great senior class is not the institutional frisbee knowledge, but the leadership knowledge.

Since it sounds like you are working without a coach, the first thing I would suggest is to put together a leadership team or junta. You are looking at 5 to 7 players with a range of experience and seniority. While it is tempting to put all the most experienced people on the junta, remember that you are consciously trying to build program longevity and this means that some of your leaders need to be people who are going to be around for a few years. Because you will be picking from people who are on the younger end, it is quite likely they won't be entirely ready; that's okay.

Rather than give you a specific leadership structure or formula I'd suggest moving forward with the goal of teaching and learning leadership skills and three big guidelines. First, learning to lead requires meaningful work. You can't learn to throw a forehand just by watching someone throw one and leadership is no different. So when you think about the inexperienced leaders on your team, it isn't enough to have them just be on the committee, they need to do real work. Have them call subs or pick defenses or run drills in practices. How you chose depends a lot on the skills and needs of the team. (See below.) The second guideline is to expect mistakes. To stick with the forehand analogy, no one throws perfectly the first time they are shown how. It takes practice, work and mistakes. Don't dwell on them, but use each as a chance to get better. The third and perhaps most important guideline is to talk and talk and talk some more. You will need to sort out who is doing what, how to do it, evaluate mistakes, make strategic decisions. Essentially, you are embarking on democracy and democracy isn't efficient. So expect to put in heaps of time in leadership meetings, phone calls, pre- and post-practice conversations.

35
MINI WITH ZOMBIES

On middle school games

Published September 11, 2013

Hi Lou,

I volunteer as an ultimate frisbee coach at a middle school in Cambridge, MA, and one thing I'm keen to help the kids with is improving their field awareness. Mainly I'm thinking about from the perspective of a thrower with the disc. Some kids (some adults too, for that matter) seem to be afflicted with tunnel vision: they lock on to one person and fail to see poaching players on defense. Do you know of any good drills to run in practice that help promote field awareness, seeing the entire field at once, identifying the poacher and the poachee, etc.?

Thanks,
Shane

Shane,

This is a very difficult and sophisticated skill to learn. The challenge is to see everything while looking for something in particular. Another way to think of this challenge is that you want your players to see the entire field without an agenda, but if they have no agenda at all, they can't make a judgement about what is a good choice. The trick is to fold your agenda into one of the things that you are observing along with the cutters, defenders, poachers, weather....

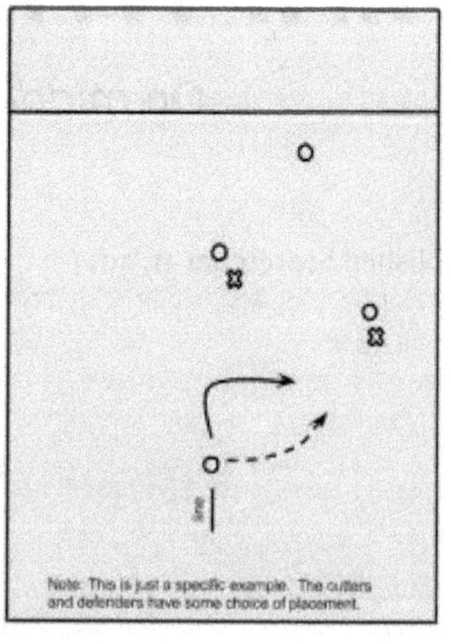

It would take a very sophisticated middle schooler to think that deeply, so here are a couple of drills. The first is a simple cut, read and throw drill illustrated in the diagram at right. The purpose of the drill is to train the eyes and mind to look at the whole field and make a decision immediately after catching the disc. There is a single line that initiates the action with a crossing pattern cut that runs about 5-yards deep. Downfield there are three offensive players and two defenders. The offensive players are spread out across the field in 'cutting' locations; as the throw goes up to the initiating crossing pattern, the defenders choose to cover two of the three offensive players. Upon the catch the thrower looks up, reads who is open and throws it to them.

The second drill is a fun one for middle school kids – it is called Zombie Defenders. This drill has multiple purposes. It practices quick, creative handler movement and reading open spaces as cutters and throwers. Set up a Mini field and prepare the teams to play 3 vs Everyone Else. The three are going to play regular ultimate and use a (creative) handler weave to advance the disc down the field.

The Everyone Else are zombies; they can't run or jump and there are lots of them. If you are doing this with middle schoolers, they probably need more guidance about what defines acceptable zombie behavior, (but will also enjoy acting like zombies). This is an easy drill to be successful with if you can see the space and therefore good practice.

A last bit of advice is to adopt some sort of keyword like "see" or "scan" that cues the behavior practiced in the drill. Have the players yell this as they initiate the behavior (the step on the cut in drill number one, for example.) This emphasizes the learning and gives you something useful to yell from the sideline during games. Good luck and a big thanks for coaching middle schoolers.

36
UNDERDOG

On beating goliath

Published September 25, 2013

Lou,

What advice would you give a team going into a game against a superior opponent? If the other team does everything better than you, what gives you the best shot at pulling off the upset?

Not the Favorite

NtF,

The most important thing is to manage expectations – which are delicate and dangerous things. On the one hand, you are unlikely to win this kind of game, so expecting to win is kind of stupid. At the same time, it isn't a very good long term strategy to make excuses for defeat – you are just setting up a situation where losing is okay. It is a very tricky line to walk – a kind of double think is necessary – and above all a crystal clear view of where you are and where you want to be.

These kind of mental gymnastics are for long term team building; what about trying to win a game in a crucial situation where you are completely outgunned? We are halfway between the two Regionals weekends here in the States, so there are lots of teams finding themselves in this spot.

The most important piece is to take advantage of your opportunities. Whether is a rash of miscues early that let you steal a lot of breaks or weak defense that lets you hang around late into the game, there is a necessary element of luck. (If your 'superior opponent' hits on all cylinders, you will lose.)

Team-wide, you want to emphasize defense. Any upset game becomes a test of mental strength and pressure as the favorite ramps up the effort and makes a push to victory. 95% of the time the inferior team can't keep pace and fades away down the stretch. Emphasizing defense allows you to generate pressure of your own and also lets you keep your focus on the positive, even as you go through a patch of struggles.

Substitute loose early. You will win this game on the back of your stars, but you can't play them the whole way and expect to hold on at the end. If you play them the whole way, you set the other team up to pull away from you – right as your opponent begins to make their push, your stars are tired and you've got no headroom to step up into. By playing fairly open early, your stars are rested and ready to play point after point after point down the stretch, improving your play as theirs improves.

Strategize for your opponent. In many of these situations you have the advantage of knowing your opponent very well – better in fact, than they know you. Good teams get filmed, their players get noticed and watched. You don't have to get all crazy and invent some special defense; on the contrary, sticking to what you do well is likelier to be effective. The best adjustments are little ones to the game plan you already have. Things like defined match-ups, which defenders not to test, knowledge of pull plays and offensive tendencies are invaluable and can make a huge difference.

36
NATIONALS Q & A

On 2013 Nationals

Published October 30, 2013

After last week's recap, I went through the comments and my email inbox and pulled questions. I also jumped some comment threads that needed expansion or further discussion.

FURY'S DEFEAT?

Before we start, let's give Scandal some credit. Payne, Jorgenson and Mercier brought it. Alicia White was dominant and Kath Ratcliff provided sneaky offensive support. The entire team played with an exuberant recklessness and nowhere was this more apparent than in their stifling defense. Great work.

This from Mike Lommler: *Speaking of Fury's defense in the final, it seemed to me that one of their greatest failings was consistently permitting Octavia Payne the space to rip upwind backhands, particularly with Jorgenson streaking deep. Even when Opi didn't complete those bombs they re-set the field position and forced Fury to face that powerful Scandal d-line for the full 70.*

I agree and on a windy day, this is a fundamental mistake…typically. In at least two of their titles (the epic Riot comeback game and again last year), Fury let the other team play field position and then calmly and patiently converted their opportunities even when they had to go 70 to do it. Overall though, Fury's defense was lacking in this game. Too often, Fury defenders were trailing cutters by two, three or four steps and yielding easy unders. It had the look of a team that was waiting to be given opportunities rather than one that was out to generate turnovers. Obviously, they had trouble with Jorgenson, but that doesn't mean the rest of the Scandal shouldn't get fronted.

This from 'Guest': *Forcing errant throw after errant throw is not the usual Alex Snyder game plan (at all) but that's what was happening and yet fury kept playing her instead of putting in younger, faster, different handlers. When something is going that wrong like it was for Furys offense that game something needed to change and for being such a high level, prestigious coach like Matty is I was very shocked and frustrated in his coaching during that final.*

The sentiment that Alex and Matty somehow let Fury down has been widely circulated, but count me a sceptic. No one on Fury played well and it is really difficult to pinpoint one individual who particularly struggled. Across the board Fury's handlers had far too many short-field swing and dump pass turnovers, but they weren't all Alex. There are complex structural and strategic issues at play here. Fury has a talent glut at handler with Hall of Famers and rising stars competing (Snyder, Casey, Sun, Fajardo, Nazarov, Finney, Sherwood) for a mere three handler spots under Fury's strict offensive. Credit Scandal's defense, particularly on the cutters. How often did Fury string together cutter to cutter throws? Too many times, Fury would hit a comeback cut, then have to throw multiple swing passes before hitting another. The numbers on a windy day just don't play out. Scandal's timely zone sneak attack only exacerbated the issue. The nail in the coffin was all around poor play from a great team. We are so used to Fury being the beneficiary of another team's mistakes we are all shocked when the script flips.

Even so, I think all the second guessers are wrong about the decisions Fury made. They've won seven in a row by staying the course, making small adjustments and calmly going about business. Over the years, Fury has turned games on little adjustments and for that Matty has relied on Alex. It is very, very difficult to take the words of a coach and turn them into action on the field. At issue is the very nature of the brain. Words are conscious thought, the very enemy of unconscious, "in-the-zone" play and it is the rare player who can take words and turn them into action. Alex can and Matty has relied on it. That's who they are and how they've gone about winning. The scorpion must sting the frog. When Fury used this plan to come back from 1-11 versus Riot it was genius, why is it a mistake now?

GOAT AND NEMESIS

From mottsauce: *Not much has been made of GOAT's collapse (and Nemesis', for that matter). What do you think are the reasons that occurred? Peaking too early? Did they mismanage personnel? Something else entirely?*

A lot of GOAT and Nemesis' 'collapses' has to do with expectations. Going in to the tournament, these teams had been anointed contenders based on a very small body of work, really just a handful of games in each case. In truth, in a landscape dominated by parity, they'd come out on the top of some close games where the W ended up weighing more in people's minds than actual performance or talent. Subzero and Sockeye went to Nationals knowing they could beat GOAT; the same was true for Showdown and Traffic and Nemesis. The same wasn't true for Revolver. Truck and PoNY went into their pool planning to lose to Revolver. Additionally, both GOAT and Nemesis suffered from a lot of film for their competitors and from the switch to hunted instead of hunter. Nationals might have been the first time everyone was out to beat them; no one went to the ProFlight Finale saying "We've got to game plan for GOAT."

In a land of parity, it is little things that make the difference between winning and losing. The lists below are deficiencies to reflect where these teams struggled, but both teams are quite good and did a lot of things right as well.

FOR GOAT:

• Their offense was stagnant. Far too often, they'd get one downfield pass and then have to swing the disc multiple times before getting another downfield shot.

• Their deep game was off. Half of their 8 turnovers in the Sockeye game came from hucks.

• Derek Alexander was off. At the end of day one, he was sitting at 12 turnovers. That's 4 per game! GOAT's formula was high percentage offense and it was built around Alexander's ability to possess and distribute.

• Sockeye's deep game was on. Rehder had five goals in the first half and two other goals came from hucks to Phil Murray.

• GOAT's expectations got the better of them. They planned to play open the first two games and then tighten up for the Sockeye game. Having chalked the first to games as wins, they neglected to tell Subzero and Madcow.

FOR NEMESIS:

• Their zone offense was terrible. On a windless day, why do you have four handlers back? Actually, why would you ever have four handlers back? Nemesis struggled to move the disc against a Showdown zone that was very weak around the edges – twenty yards down the sideline was there for the taking.
• Their defense overplayed the open side. In the Showdown game, the Texans were able to get easy flow and easy goals working down the breakside/strongside after an initial break. This was particularly evident after Texas put away their struggling horizontal and went almost exclusively vert in the second two-thirds.
• Cara Crouch did whatever she wanted. Really. Johnson is a great player and defender, but she isn't enough alone to deal with Cara. Some help defense would have been nice.
• Nemesis' d team failed to convert their early opportunities.

FORMAT

Also from mottsauce: *"Now that we have, do you think this is an improvement over the prior format or not? The win-or-go-home prequarters matchups between the 2 and 3 seeds were fantastic (Chain/Truck, Traffic/Capitals, and Machine/Pony) and the format opens up more doors for "underdog" teams (Showdown and Sockeye breaking seed are the two easy examples) to advance when compared to simply eliminating the three weakest teams from the two lower power pools."*

Strategically, the formula for winning is play well in pool play so you can rest your studs, then play them like crazy down the stretch. No one executed this better than Revolver (who probably benefited from a light schedule early). No team seemed interested in gaming the system by throwing games. Partly, this has to do with the makeup of club teams.

Unlike the college division, where teams are very reliant on a handful of players and throwing games is standard practice at Regionals, club teams are much deeper. They can stay with their regular strategies and not overly tax their stars, particularly if they are winning and can keep their offense off the field.

I'd still like to see some adjustments to the format. Eliminate the 1-4 pre quarters game. Win your pool, go to quarters. Lose your pool, go home. There are so many exciting games on the second day; it was a tragedy they were all crammed into the morning. Spread the round of 16 and the quarters out so that more of those games are available for fans. On a side note, too much is made of the format 'exploiting' players. Play late and start early? Not a big deal, just a new challenge to overcome; like any challenge there are good strategies for dealing with it.

MAKING SEMIS

From Joaqman: *"In the last 20 years only 4 open teams failed to make the semifinals after winning the championship the previous year: Condors 2002*, Sockeye 2008*, Jam 2009, and Doublewide 2013. Is there a reason for the consecutive examples in the late aughts or is it just coincidence? Is it harder now to maintain or is it just WUGC Sockeye (they got back to semis in 2009), then two teams that happened to experience key retirements post championship?"*

The jump from quarters to semis is the hardest jump in ultimate. In any given year, there are 2-4 truly great teams and 6-10 good teams. Those six to ten good teams have a pretty high likelihood of making quarters – there are eight spots and they only need one of them. Additionally, they only need to beat another good team to get there. But to make semifinals, you often have to beat a great team, which a good team rarely, rarely ever does. Add in the travails the 7 and 8 seeds endured under the old power pool play in game system and the odds get even slimmer.

One of the reasons that so few champions have failed to make the subsequent semifinals is that most teams stay great and great teams don't lose, but I'll take these five champs on one by one.

CONDORS 2002. The Sockeye-Condors power pool game was one of the most physically intense games I've been a part of at Nationals. It was the first 'hot' Nationals and no one was prepared to deal with the 90 degree temperatures, let alone two Mild Coast teams. Both the Fish and the Condors went on to lose their next challenging game.

SOCKEYE 2008. An overly ambitious season (Dream Cup, Worlds and Nationals), a giant and diffuse roster and a Bravo team in the quarters that finally managed to get the monkey (Fish) off its back. And score was 14-13.

JAM 2009. This wasn't the same team that won in 2008.

CHAIN 2010. Chain's title in 2009 is looking more and more like an aberration in a landscape dotted with quarterfinal exits. I think the real question is not why did they lose, but how did they win?

DOUBLEWIDE 2013. In a deep field, they lost two close games to eventual semifinalists. From what I saw, they never felt or played with the urgency and intensity from their 2012 campaign. At least until the end of the Bravo game. If they'd played with that fervor the whole tournament, who knows how things might have turned out.

MLU

From Bjorn Schey: *"What does it mean that Boston won MLU against SF in light of their semis exit in USAU?"*

Not much. Most of the elite players still view MLU and AUDL as a pleasant off-season diversion. The Club Championships are still the single most difficult tournament in the world and the winner is still the best team in the world. That may change at some point in the future, but not for a few years yet.

From Charlie: *"On a side note, I am also interested in what you think (or if you think) that the explosion of MLU and the AUDL had any Impact on the TCT this season– it seemed as if there was significantly less of a hangover from the respective seasons than in 2012 (ex, southpaw winning in AUDL, but not qualifying for nationals."*

The semi-pro teams helped those cities prepare earlier and develop new talent. That early development was most on display at the US Open where Boston and San Francisco were clearly ahead of the MLU-less Triangle and Austin. I didn't see Southpaw's failure as an AUDL hangover, I don't think they were very good and their AUDL domination was more about the third-tier status of AUDL year one than anything that Southpaw did particularly well.

BOSTON

From Guest: *"You might be too hard on Boston. Look at the 3-3 point in the semis: Clark has the disc on the goal line after a foul, and his dump to Markette is dropped. Sockeye (eventually) scores. They lost by one point, and here was one play where they score 95 times out of 100. I don't know what happens if they had played Revolver in the finals, though."*

I don't think I am as hard on them as they are being on themselves. For the last six years, they have entered the season as legitimate title contenders. This season, they came in as the preseason favorites. But this isn't just what the press and the chattering classes think – this is what they think internally. If your goal is winning and you don't…. it's really hard to take. I was a part of the Sockeye teams that lost repeatedly to DoG (late 90s) and then Furious (early 00s) before finally breaking through. Those years were incredibly, incredibly difficult. Ironically, the only team that really and truly suffered for years and came through intact to win it all? Boston's Death or Glory.

THE BIGGEST LOSER

In all this discussion of on the field action, the biggest change to the frisbee landscape almost went by unnoticed and unmentioned (except on Twitter). The biggest loser from the shift in Nationals? The Daiquiri Deck. Although something will come along to replace it, traditions are part of what make ultimate special and like the passing of the Palm Bay, the passing of the Saturday night at the Daiquiri Deck is something we should take a moment and mourn.

37
CASH ON THE TABLE

On available game time

Published December 11, 2013

One of the ways I approach developing strategy is the idea of 'cash on the table.' This principle of economics and biology states that if there are untapped opportunities or resources, someone or something will come along and take advantage of them. That's why there are many, many things that like to eat road kill. Because ultimate is so young, there are still a lot of these opportunities. Oregon's weird zone and fast break offense are good examples of this.

Shifts in the rules also offer opportunities. Last spring, the Wisconsin men were huddling on offense until right before the 20 second warning, greatly reducing the amount of time the opposing defense had to match up.

In the spirit of Christmas, here's an unused idea. (Full disclosure: I couldn't get it to work in the women's game.) I often borrow ideas from other sports and this one came from football. I was watching a game, one team punted and promptly gave up a punt return for a touchdown. The broadcasters lamented that the kicking team had 'out-kicked their coverage' and I realized that every team in ultimate routinely out-kicks their coverage. Think for a moment about the best pulls – they hang forever, sit deep and allow the defense an opportunity to set up before the first pass. Think for a moment – how many offenses are built around a free first pass? With a little practice, it should be possible to time your pull and your defenders and get them in sync. Instead of having your manliest man throw it as far as he can, work on the timing and flight of the pull to coincide with the arrival of the defenders. You will have to give up 5-10 yards on the pull, but you were giving those yards up already because the other team was getting a free first pass. Take it, it's yours.

38
THE INNER GAME OF DRILLS

On drilling

Published February 5, 2014

I was wondering what you feel are the best pre-game warm drills/exercises to run.

Before I get to specific drills, here are some general guidelines to keep in mind.

- Your entire warm up sequence should be designed to prepare you to play physically and mentally. No individual drill will do this and the overall sequence and pace of warm-ups are more important.

• People typically over-emphasize the physical aspect of warmups and ignore or neglect the mental. A good warmup is a ritual that prepares your mind for the coming competition.

• You want to progress from 70% effort up to 100% and then back down to 90% just before game time.

• As much as you can, physically prepare with a disc in hand. If you wait until you are 100% warm to touch a frisbee, you've lost a lot of repetitions.

• Consider splitting your team in half for disc drills. This doubles your touches per minute. I recommend this all the way down to teams of 12. Six people is plenty to run most warm-up drills. Long lines are a brutal waste of time.

• Design a warm up that fits your style of play. Are you a hucking team? Spend more time on this. Are you a defensive team? Spend more time on footwork drills.

Here are some of my personal favorites:

• 3-person marking drill. This is the best single drill in ultimate. It emphasizes the most important foundational two skills – marking and breaking the mark – it is competitive and physically demanding. What's not to like?

• 20 minutes of unstructured throwing. This is a tough drill for younger players because they don't really know how to use twenty minutes and often devolve into chat-throwing, but for your veterans and big-time throwers, twenty minutes to throw is wonderful. By the end of my time with Sockeye, I had 8-10 throws I expected to use every game and another 8-10 I might use. (This is not atypical for club-level throwers.) It takes a while to warm all those up, suss out the weather conditions and mental framework.

• A progression of straight on to straight on + cut to straight on + cut + marker. This is a lovely build from 80% to 90% to 100% intensity. Like the 3-person marking drill, it emphasizes foundational skills – throwing, marking, cutting, catching. If you've split your team, you can get 10-20 reps in a very short amount of time.

• Oregon's hammer drill. The motion is a simple flare-cut, hammer, flare-cut, blade. In addition to practicing the most under-utilized throw in women's ultimate, it's a great catching drill for warming up hands and feet. Taking this back to the guidelines above, this drill is also a perfect fit for how we want to play offense – loose, carefree and unconventional.

39

FORCE MIDDLE

On forcing middle

Published January 15, 2014

I love force middle but find it hard to teach the downfield defenders where to be, especially against a ho stack. Who's covering the deep space? Who's marking under? Etc. I find it hard to explain to people when the disc moves to a sideline. When you're coaching this, what do you say to your defenders to make them understand where to be and how to generate pressure and turns? And what drills do you do to work on them? Any advice on this would be appreciated.

Matt

Before I get into too much detail, there are a couple really important things to realize about force middle. First, you are already playing force middle some of the time. When you are playing force forehand as a defense and you are on the backhand side of the field forcing forehand, you're forcing the middle of the field. A lot of the same concepts you use defensively in this situation apply in force middle. The difficulty for most people comes on the switch from one force to the other. The biggest difficulty for most people, though, is how uncomfortable force middle makes them. If you have only ever played force-one-way, the constantly switching mark, the variability of the positioning and the open side vulnerability are really unsettling for a lot of people. If you are going to teach force middle, you really have to stick with it through a weeks or months long period of dislike.

The idea of force middle is to double cover the strong side of the field with the marker and the defender putting pressure on the throwing lane right in front of the disc. Force middle is very vulnerable to cross field throws, typically swings and big banana-hucks. It isn't a particularly good defense against horizontal stack because the middle of the field is so open. It is a much better defense against vert stack because the stack plays defense on the middle of the field. If you play force middle you should be prepared to give up more swings, but fewer big passes. If a typical force forehand possession averages 5 passes per possession and zone 10, you'd expect force middle to fall in the 7-8 range.

From a teaching angle, here are the things I emphasize:

- Get the mark on right away. The downfield defenders are briefly exposed on almost every pass and need the help.

- Repositioning is essential. Look on the up call, get the information you need (catch spot, thrower, marking situation) and get yourself into the right spot.

• Play head up. More so than in a force one way, force middle requires constant repositioning which requires constant information. Keep your head up. Keep looking around.

• Overplay the strong side. (Vocabulary note: strong side = disc side and is independent from open side.) On the sideline, this means covering the inside-out lane and leaving the big swing to the weak side of the field open.

• As in all defenses, you can play tight or loose as a matter of preference. If you want to help, the two spots to work from against a horizontal are off the handler and the weak-side deep. Against a vert, it's against the handler again and the mid-stack cutters.

You had a couple of specific questions that I haven't hit yet, Matt. Regarding who covers the deep vs. under space, the 'on-stage' defenders must cover the under, otherwise you will be bled a slow death ten yards at a go. They can't entirely cede the out, which is the challenge of being the on-stage defender. I would suggest bringing a defender off the weak side to help over the top. This isn't really an FM thing, but a defense thing. As for pressure, FM is a more conservative defense than one-way, so much of the pressure comes from pushing the other team past their comfort level for possession and progress. The blocks come from the offense either trying to squeeze something into a tight window or off of a long weak side throw. To explain a bit further, FM gives up throws across the field. This gives the defense a long run at the disc, so even though they may initially be out of position, they have a lot of opportunity to force a play.

Finally, some drill suggestions:

• I like running two and three person situations.

• Example 1: to work on getting the mark on you can run a set that starts with a gimme 20 yard swing. The defense's job is to pursue and contain by getting the mark on.

• Example 2: a three person situation where the two handlers throw gimme swings back and forth and the downfield defender works on repositioning to the new circumstances.

• Notice that these are simple and work on a single skill. Begin with these and then work to more complex situations. Generally speaking, people try to make defensive drills too 'real' too soon, before the foundational skills are solid.

40

IT'S ABOUT THE TEAM

On captainship

Published January 22, 2014

Q: You may have read the article on Ultiworld recently about the best traits in a captain. Maybe you could address this in your next Win the Fields? What traits do you look for as a coach and what traits did you look for as a player? Any resources for captains in ultimate or from other sports?

A: Kummer pretty much hits the nail on the head with this article, so I don't want to try to replicate his work. Rather, I'd like to look forward to how you can avoid some of these difficulties and create a sin-free captaincy. I would also expand the scope of this article to include coaches. One of the things we really try for at Oregon is equality of leadership – the captains and I work in partnership.

No one person can do all of this stuff; all captains and coaches have flaws. For years, organization and logistics was my Achilles heel. I've gotten better, but I always delegated all that stuff – tourney fees, vans, hotels. Not out of laziness, but a recognition that I was too inconsistent for a task that requires daily attention to detail. The best way for a team to manage the inevitable gaps in leadership is to select a range of personality and skills into the captaincy. So you may end up with one player who is great with logistics, another who is great on the field and in the huddle and a third who really understands people. Individually, they'd have major flaws, but collectively they are complete. You can even delegate some of this stuff outside of the captaincy. There's no reason your sub caller has to be a captain or that a captain has to design the offense. Use the skills the team has – the captains' job is to make sure things are getting done – it doesn't matter by who. There is one job that must be done by a captain – it's one that I (in homage to Elvis) call the TCB, Taking Care of Business. Every day, every week, every practice, every drill there are things that have to be done. A meeting needs to be arranged, the team needs a kick in the pants to start warming up, someone needs a one-on-one about attitude…it is endless. You need someone on the team to pay attention to these things, see them and then make sure they are dealt with.

The essential idea of this article is that it's not about you, it's about the team. I couldn't agree more. The easy part is giving away time, energy and effort. Harder, but more important, is giving away being right. As an example, one of your best defenders won't run the offense after the turn. (Which is a bad thing.) As a non-captain, you can complain and grumble as much as you want. This kind of grumbling is not good, but it happens on a lot of teams and the people who are grumble are right – she should run the offense and not free-lance. As a captain, though, you don't have the luxury of complaining; you need to get her to run the offense. Everyone is motivated differently and you will often have to be flexible on the means you use to change her behavior because it is the ends that matter.

As for resources, outside of Rise Up, there aren't a lot out there that are ultimate specific. I certainly hope this blog is helpful in some capacity; that's a big piece of why I write. (Shameless plug: send in your questions!) Despite the dearth of frisbee resources, there are an enormous amount of non-frisbee resources: books, videos, blogs… it's endless really. This is probably a good problem to crowd source; if you've got recommendations of coaching resources, throw them in the comments.

~

THE SHERMANATOR

Richard Sherman's antics are going to help the Seahawks win the Superbowl. The two week run up to the Superbowl is an absurd media explosion, an intense public pressure that blows away anything any of these professional athletes has ever experienced. Every player will respond to this in different ways: some will revel in it, some will be destroyed by it, some will both revel and get destroyed. The advantage the Seahawks have is a lightning rod known as Richard Sherman. He loves the attention, loves the talking and plays better the more attention and talking there is. In a world of boring 'one game at a time' and 'I followed coach's game plan' interviews, Sherman's interviews stand out for their honesty, both entertaining and ugly. The national media loves it. A quick look at SI Tuesday morning showed 5 of the first 6 headlines are about Sherman. Facebook and Twitter were blowing up. He just gets stronger. At the same time, he is insulating the rest of his team from the scrutiny. Every reporter standing around waiting for him to say something is one who isn't bugging Michael Coleman or KJ Wright.

What's this got to do with ultimate? The Richard Shermans of ultimate, the guys (and it's usually guys) who spike and talk trash and argue calls and argue other people's calls are doing their team a service. Like Richard Sherman, they're catching all the flack and static, thus shielding their team.

While we're on the Seahawks, let me quote Pete Carroll:

> *"I told them this weekend, we don't let them be themselves, we celebrate them being themselves, and we cheerlead for them to be themselves. And we try to bring out the best that they have to offer. Sometimes we go overboard, sometimes the individual gets out of bounds, and you have to step back and get back in bounds. I understand that. That's kind of how we operate. It may sound different to you, but that's how we do it. I'm trying to help our team be great and play great football and do this game the way we're supposed to do it. I don't want to miss out on somebody because maybe they're not like me. I'm OK with that."*

I've spent years trying to explain Clown Tent and along comes smarmy So-Cal Pete Carroll to do it for me. What a strange, unexpected world.

41

WHAT DO YOU EXPECT

On playing good defense

Published January 29, 2014

Let's set aside athleticism and intensity for a minute. If you want to play good defense, these are non-negotiable. While there are ways to improve each, I'd like to focus on some of the 'soft' defensive skills that are often overlooked.

The first is what I've always called the Rolodex. As you develop as a defender, you come to know other players better and better. Once you know what someone's strengths and tendencies are you can leverage your play to deny them their strengths and force them into their weaknesses. Everyone does this to some extent; the current classic example is forcing Beau under and making him a thrower. This is a really, really obvious example but there are subtle ways of affecting any player's game. You can develop the ability to quickly analyze another player. Begin with your own teammates. You see them a lot, so you know them well. Then move on to opponents you play often. As you expand the number of players you've Rolodexed, you'll find it easier to Rolodex new people.

The second piece is developing the awareness to control offensive players. Most cuts are won well before the cut starts – the cutting is just the finishing off what was already established during the set-up. Situational awareness is essential here because it allows you to play your opponent to maximum effect. To use Beau again as an example, you can actually afford to front him when certain Revolver players have the disc, because they never, never huck it. But if Ashlin is getting it, you'd better respect the deep. Circumstances extend beyond players as well – wind, the mark, how the thrower is receiving the disc – all have major impact on what will happen next and how you want to set up.

The actual application of these soft skills is mostly footwork with a dash of looking-around added in. I'd recommend a lot of agility work: cone drills and serpentines. (There are so many free on-line resources for this sort of thing, but I don't have one that I like enough to recommend.) When you are scrimmaging, mark up on players who are going to be a slight, but not impossible, challenge. Focus on denying them what they want; use your footwork to drive them into their weakness.

42
UNTITLED

On tragedy

Published March 5, 2014

Throughout the last week, my heart has been very much with the families, friends and teammates. And also with all the people who suffer through more private but no less painful tragedies.

Words have flown and with them joy.
They gathered wings and were gone.

Who knew so much grief could travel through this little thing I hold in my hand?

Words and words and words. So many people I know speak so beautifully. I am anger and incoherence. I grope in the dark and find nothing.

All day on the field I think "This is where they should be." In the huddles, I have no words, so the team holds hands. At the end of the day, the rain lifts and it is beautiful. Clouds soar above the Coast Range; the smog is all washed away and everything is clean. I try to really see it. I wish they were here to see it.

I come home. I still can't speak. I go into the darkened room and gently push sweaty locks of hair back from small, sleeping faces. I think of their mothers doing the same thing. In the morning, I stay too long at home. I will be late for work.

I know words will come back eventually. I know joy will come back eventually.

They will return when we aren't looking at the sky.

I will wake up and hear them calling in the trees.

One day, friends will wake up and hear them calling in the trees.

One day, mothers and fathers will wake up and hear them calling in the trees.

The sound will be different, darker and purple, but they will call.

43
YOUR TALENTED INTUITION

On talent hotbeds and stats

Published February 12, 2014

I'm an avid reader of your column, a middle school teacher and administrator, and coach in Seattle. You might be familiar with The Marshall Memo, a weekly digest of educational research and practice. Daniel Coyle's article How Talent Can Be Grown caught my eye, and thought that it could be neat to talk about in a "Win the Fields" bit. Would love your view of it.

A little backstory first: Daniel Coyle is the author of the Talent Code.

His basic idea is that talent can be taught and that there is a commonality about how really great talent is taught. The commonalities that he found when he looked at "talent hot-beds" around the world are:

- Ignition – An event or role model that provides powerful motivation to work hard and a belief that excellent performance is achievable.

- Master coaching – These teachers are "talent whisperers" who help develop a love for doing something, fuel passion, inspire deep practice, and bring out the best in students.

- Deep practice – Hard, sustained work at the outer limits of one's current ability, developing physical or mental skill to the next level.

In a lot of ways, this isn't particularly revolutionary – motivation, great coaching and quality practice are three obvious ingredients to success.

One of the things that he discusses a lot– but without explicitly naming it– is the importance of a culture of excellence. Let's run a little thought experiment: take two freshman ultimate players who find the sport through a club sports fair. Our first player lands on a team that is struggling for numbers, has a local club player who kind of helps out sometimes and no real plan for improvement. Our second player happens into a big-time program – 20+ players, a great coach and a directed, focused plan. Who is more motivated to improve? Who is more likely to have her efforts directed in a positive way? Knowing that your work will pay off is incredibly motivating, and a culture of excellence makes that path clearer and more possible.

I also really like the idea of 'deep practice.' This is where growth happens. All too often, we fall into comfortable and non-challenging patterns that do nothing to make us better. The classic example of this is the way in which players warm their throws up before a game. How often do you see people playing beach Frisbee, casually tossing the disc back and forth and chatting? You shouldn't fool yourself that 'deep practice' is easy or easy to get to. It requires an incredible amount of mental energy to make this type of practice happen. Almost all of Coyle's examples are of people who are 'professionals' at whatever they are practicing. (I am using professional here in the sense that their practice is the number one priority in their life.) In the Talent Code video, he talked about the kind of practice kids get at these special tennis and music schools. These kids are functionally professionals. Most ultimate players are not. We are students and parents, teachers and IT nerds, and almost all of us are coming to ultimate as a secondary activity. I can tell you from experience 'deep practice' is really, really hard to pull off in the three hours between work and family. You can do it, though. The trick is to compartmentalize so that you have a mental place to go, a particular mental state that you slip into when you get to practice. This mental space is one where 'deep practice' is the norm.

Last week, someone asked for resource recommendations on coaching, leadership and personal growth. I didn't really have a source of continuing information, but I'd add Coyle's blog. The things he's thinking about – building talent – are the things we are wondering about.

~

I wanted to take a moment to riff on statistics. I ran into this article on advanced analytics on Grantland. Basically, the idea is that if you have enough data and enough processing power you can assign a value to every possible state (set of positions) for an NBA game. If you compare a particular state to an 'optimal state' you can assign a relative value to players positioning and performance. This idea, that through the miracle of big data and processing you can assign some 'real value' to a player is incredibly appealing. And incredibly hollow. Even the authors are skeptical:

> *On the quest for the perfect analytical device, the first discovery should always be the inescapable fact that there is no perfect analytical device. There is no singular metric that explains basketball any more than there is a singular metric that explains life. It's hard not to improperly elevate the role of "big data" in contemporary sports analyses, but romanticizing them is dangerous. Data are necessarily simplified intermediaries that unite performances and analyses, and the world of sports analytics is built upon one gigantic codec that itself is built upon the defective assumption that digits can represent athletics.*

One of the flaws in this system is that it fails to account for ecology. Sports strategy, tactics and performance exist within an ecology where certain offenses and defenses are more prevalent. We are currently in a transitional phase as we leave the horizontal dominated era and move to something new. (I am not sure if we are going back to vert or if we are moving to a richer, more complicated ecosystem where teams employ different strategies. I am inclined to the latter, but time will tell.) The value of certain states has been assessed using historical data that assumes an ecology that no longer exists. Take a look at the Seahawks — credit their defense with being great, but also credit it with being great in the current pass-happy NFL. Swap them with the '86 Bears and I don't think either defense is as good.

I am even more skeptical given the framework we operate from in ultimate. We don't have SportsVu camera tracking every moment. We don't have giant processors cranking all the data. Even with all that set aside, I am still deeply distrustful of statistics. Now, don't get me wrong, I use statistics a lot. I like to track the basics and do some rudimentary analysis, but these are only a tiny part of deciding how to proceed. Statistics should be a piece of your overall evaluation, along with video working and just watching. In a lot of ways, statistics point you to questions and places to look. Barbara Hoover is catching 40% of UW's goals? Why? And then you go to the film or a game for the answers.

Really, I want to make the case for trusting your intuition. When you are watching and playing, you are unknowingly absorbing a huge amount of data and your subconscious is analyzing all of it. Your brain is a SportsVu and a building full of processors — let it do its work. (And I promise a lot more on this topic in a few weeks.)

44

SHUT UP WORD, MIND. I'M BUSY

On failures of the human mind

Published February 26, 2014

I recently finished Daniel Kahneman's excellent *Thinking, Fast and Slow.* The book is a journey through a career spent looking at the failures of the human mind. From the first page, I was struck by the foundational similarity between Thinking and my all-time favorite book about sports, Timothy Gallwey's *The Inner Game of Tennis.* Both books posit a split mind with one branch in charge of intuitive, rapid judgments and the other in charge of slower, more analytical judgements. Confusingly, they each call the two minds Self 1 and Self 2, but backwards. For clarity, I'll refer to the two minds as the Doing Mind (intuitive, rapid, visual) and the Word Mind (slow, analytical, judgmental).

The recognition of the split mind is pretty much where the similarity ends. Kahneman has an essentially distrustful view on people's ability to make judgements and has designed experiment after experiment to demonstrate the ways in which we mess things up. Gallwey's philosophy is much more experiential and completely oppositional to Kahneman's. Where Kahneman sees the human mind as rife with failings and prone to mistakes, Gallwey sees the mind as essentially trustworthy and exquisitely functional, provided we can channel it in the right way. What I'd like to do in this essay is look at each book individually, compare them and then examine the implications for playing and coaching.

INNER GAME

If you haven't read this book, do so today. It is the best use of the next two hours of your life. Better than track or lifting or throwing or practice. It's that good.

Inner Game begins with a recognition of two minds and the damage the Word Mind can do to athletic performance:

> *...within each player there are two "selves." One, the "I" seems to give instructions; the other, "myself" seems to perform the action. Then "I" returns with an evaluation of the action. For clarity, let's call the "teller" Self 1 [the Word Mind] and the "doer" Self 2 [the Doing Mind].*

By thinking too much and trying too hard, [the Word Mind] has produced tension and muscle conflict in the body. He is responsible for the error, but he heaps the blame on [the Doing Mind] and then, by condemning it it further, undermines his own confidence in [the Doing Mind]. As a result, the stroke grows worse and worse and frustration builds.

Once he has established the idea of the two minds, Gallwey uses the rest of the book to explain methods to avoid the dangers of this split mind and allow natural athletic ability to flourish. There are two essential steps in this process: quieting the Word Mind and trusting the Doing Mind. These steps aren't necessarily sequential because the trusting of the Doing Mind is often a key step in getting the Word Mind to be quiet.

THINKING, FAST AND SLOW

Like *Inner Game, Thinking* divides the human mind into two systems:

> *The [Doing Mind] operates automatically and quickly, with little or no effort and no sense of voluntary control. The [Word Mind] allocates attention to the effortful mental activities that demand it, including complex computations. The operations of the [Word Mind] are often associated with the subjective experience of agency, choice and concentration.*

Kahneman sees the human mind fail in multiple ways. The root of the problem is that the Doing Mind is always working and the Word Mind is lazy. No matter what you do, you cannot turn the Doing Mind off; it will always supply an answer to a question, even if it has no idea what it is talking about. This is particularly true of questions that are better answered by the Word Mind. Compounding the problem, the Word Mind requires a lot of work and effort to bring to bear. It is very resource-intensive; it tires easily; it cannot multi-task. So although it is very, very good at certain things, it is also very limited. Kahneman often sees the Word Mind fail to answer questions it should.

A common type of Doing Mind error is for the Doing Mind to

supply an answer to a different, simpler question. "Is this politician competent" (a tricky analytical question) gets replaced with "Does this politician look and sound like a leader?" There are a number of different "substitution" errors of this nature described in the book. As coaches we have things that we care about and choose to emphasize. When our teams are struggling, we are inclined to place the blame and the appropriate correction within the area we care more about. Personally, I am apt to attribute struggles to lack of effort and defense. Other coaches will attribute struggles to poor choices or execution. These things might be right, but we are substituting the question "What is making me frustrated with my team's play" for the broader "Why is my team struggling?"

There are a number of setting and framing errors described as well. One that I thought was particularly telling in ultimate was the 'halo effect'. This is an error where we make a judgement about one ability based on our observations about something else entirely. The example from ultimate that came to my mind immediately was from tryouts. Two people show up for practice; you can only pick one for the team. (This is a difficult analytical question that involves weighing a lot of different factors, a classic Word Mind question.) The first player looks the part — 5 shorts, sublimated jerseys — you know that kid. The second looks a schlub: raggedy cotton sweatshirt, bad hair. It is really, really hard to give these two a fair comparison. 5 shorts don't make you a better ultimate player, but they make you look like a better ultimate player and the Doing Mind will say that they are a better player. This is a really great argument for objective analytics at tryouts. At Oregon, we run a series of 6-8 different metrics as a part of our tryout process. In addition to the support of hard data, you also have to openly address halo effect issues in the tryout process. This is what Kahneman refers to as bringing the Word Mind into action. This is where the Word Mind is strongest – detailed, slow analysis.

IMPLICATIONS FOR PLAYERS

There is no question that the act of playing ultimate is a Doing Mind activity. I don't want to rehash what Gallwey has already said so eloquently, but the essence of it is that to be an effective player, you need to get the Word Mind to shut up and get out of the Doing Mind's way.

We already do a lot of work to get the Word Mind out of the way. The most obvious example is drill work. Running a drill is taking a new concept and by practicing it again and again moving it into the automatic, intuitive Doing Mind. Part of the difficulty is that you have to pass through a period of Word Mind work until this becomes automatic. Let's look at learning dump-swing as an example. The first time your coach or captain explains this fairly basic piece of technology, it is hard to grasp and hold all the different pieces: the initial handler does this, the second handler does that and then the weakside cutter… it goes on and on. You have a million what-if questions. You get into the drill and completely muck it up. You are trying to remember to time your cut and forget what to do when the initial handler goes up the line. You get yelled at. But as you do the drill more and more, it becomes more and more automatic. You get into a game and without being told what to do, the dump-swing just happens. It's like magic. But it isn't magic, it's just how we learn. It's the Doing Mind in action.

Another way we do this work already is to prepare ourselves to play during our warm ups. As I mentioned a couple of weeks ago, your warm up should be preparing you mentally as well as physically. You are getting yourself into a frame of mind where the Word Mind shuts up and the Doing Mind takes over. This process is a slow to learn, but it is learnable skill. If you've ever been around experienced club players and watched them 'turn it on', you've seen someone who has learned how to make that switch without a lot of prep work.

A final note: the Word Mind is activated by high-stress, high-pressure moments. There isn't really anything you can do about this because it is automatic. This is why people get the yips, drop passes on game point, blow defensive assignments. All of a sudden, at the worst possible time, the Word Mind is turned on and activated. It's just trying to be helpful but it mucks everything up. The best way around this is to play in a lot of high pressure situations. This is why so many teams fail in their first trip to the Finals; experience mitigates pressure and inexperience maximizes it. You can replicate this at practice: the standard drill for this is Game to 2.

IMPLICATIONS FOR COACHES/LEADERS

Unlike the relatively straightforward problem faced by players, the issues for coaches and leaders are much more complicated. Is coaching a Doing Mind or a Word Mind activity? At first glance, it seems like it would be a Word Mind activity just because there is so much thinking involved, but as I've reflected back on my own thought process I feel more and more that coaching is largely a Doing Mind activity with an uncomfortable and awkward amount of Word Mind mixed in.

Think back on your own mental process during a game. (This is a bit like using a scale to weigh itself.) How much are you carefully weighing evidence? How much are you looking at data and extrapolating plans and strategies from this data? If you're like me, not much. So much of the work I do during a game is fast — really quick, rapid judgements. Even in a situation where I am trying to make a decision about a strategic change (it could be anything: zone to person or a change in match-ups or which pull play to run) I only have 30 seconds or at most a couple of minutes to make that decision. I'm not looking back at film, I'm not analyzing a lot of data — I'm going with my gut, which is unquestionably the Doing Mind.

I think this is true of most of the work we do. Running drills, doing player analysis, watching film…so much of this work is image-based and intuitive and so little of it involves the detailed analysis of data. This was surprising to me. I really expected coaching to be Word Mind.

This raises a really awkward problem for us as coaches and leaders. Our job as coaches is to impart our understanding to the players. How do you impart this knowledge without words? We must grapple with a brutal 4-step translation problem: Our Doing Mind to our Word Mind spoken to the players' Word Mind to the players Doing Mind. Yikes! It's no wonder we say stuff in a huddle and then watch it not happen on the field. The real surprise should be that it happens at all! (It is a poorly understood and often ignored athletic talent to translate Word to Doing. I think it's related to processing speed, but I'm not 100%.)

Here are some real practical suggestions to work around this problem:

• If you make an unpracticed, in-game adjustment expect it to go poorly. You're asking the Word Mind to play ultimate. So when you are weighing whether or not to do it, you are balancing the 'rightness' of the adjustment with the 'poorness' of the execution. As an example – you never play zone, but your person is getting killed. Zone might be the right hypothetical choice, but defenders are going to blow assignments. No choice here is good, so pick the best of the worst.

• Find the players who can translate quickly and have them make the adjustments for the whole team. In the 2011 Fury-Riot final, Matty Tsang said at halftime that he wanted to use forehand inside-outs to move the disc to the high-side of the field. Then Alex Snyder went out and threw 4-5 of these beautifully. Not all of Fury made this adjustment, but one player adjusting was enough.

• Don't talk analytical strategy right before game time. Don't turn the Word Mind on. The best way to manage this is to have your strategy conversation the night before or at the beginning of the day before you have started warm-ups. Present your strategy adjustments in a way that make them easily transferable to a few words each, like "No arounds". Your pre-game huddle is then a very brief reiteration of these key points and a lot of emotional preparation. A tactical suggestion: don't go into the pre-game huddle. Leave it to the players.

• Words are worthless. If you want something to happen, you have to drill it. And drill it again. And again. It has to transfer into the Doing Mind.

THE TOGETHER MIND

There's a stronger place than merely silencing the Word Mind. You need the Word Mind to be successful because so many of the goals of ultimate are artificial. You need the judgement seeking, external analysis of the Word Mind to create forward momentum. Without it, the Doing Mind just sits and zens itself to nowhere.

When you are really on, when you are really aware, your Doing Mind is absorbing each and every piece of information and taking it into account. The wind, the mark, the slight positioning of the defenders, the match-up…there's so much. But amazingly, the thoughts of the Word Mind become just another piece absorbed into the decision making of the Doing Mind. The score, the number of time-outs, these just become another piece of information added in.

There is a place even beyond this, where both the Word and Doing Mind are fully active. I've been there once. In the 2004 finals, I was fortunate enough to be on the field for Sockeye on double game point. We forced a turnover and I had to walk the disc up to the front cone with 70 yards to go. Twice. The first time it happened, I had an out of body experience where a part of me was watching from above as I walked the disc to the line. The watching-me thought, "Holy shit, you're walking the disc into coffin corner on double game point in the finals of Nationals!" But the rest of me, the active me, the part of me that was in my body just stepped up and threw the swing pass. The second time it happened, I had the same out of body experience, complete with the same internal monologue. And again I threw the swing pass.

CONCLUSION

To bring this back to Kahneman and Gallwey, they're actually in agreement. They see the human mind exactly the same. They each agree that the human mind has its flaws and its strengths. They agree that the challenge that faces us is to attack the situation in front of us in an appropriate way. Gallwey spent a life on the tennis courts watching and teaching. It is no surprise he favors the Doing Mind. Kahneman spent his life in the halls of academia wondering about errors in judgement and statistical analysis. This is Word Mind work. Their works themselves reflect their favored Mind. *Inner Game* is succinct and thematic; *Thinking* is meticulous, detailed and long.

The next stop for me will be to look more closely at the expert mind. Gary Klein's *Sources of Power* is likely. What I am seeking is how we can learn to see something immensely complex (like an ultimate game) in a coherent manner. I have struggled lately with the realization that what I see on the field is not what the players see. This should be obvious, but it hadn't occurred to me. Now I struggle with how to impart that vision.

45
THE CUTTING TREE

On cutting and staying at the top of the game

Published March 12, 2014

You have mentioned in the past about how much work Mike Caldwell put in during an offseason to truly elevate his game to the elite level, and talked about him running the "cutting tree" again and again. What exactly is the cutting tree, and is there a way to effectively teach that to a team?

The most impressive thing about MC's game is how self-made it is. There are certain talents that silver-spoon their way into elite ultimate;

maybe they're tall, maybe they're fast. Maybe they had a star-crossed juniors career that set them up early. Good for those people, but I've always had a soft spot for those of us (and it's most of us) who really, really have to work for every little step up the mountain. That's the path Mike took from his freshman year with GOP to throwing two Greatests in national title games.

When I got this question, I immediately sent it on to Mike. Why would I answer it when he can tell it better? What's great about what Mike has to say is that it is a path anyone can take – a blueprint for the blue-collar. Enjoy.

Get four cones. Set them up in a square, 15 to 20 yards on each side. On one side, walk the cones in a couple yards to make a parallelogram.

Imagine these as points on a field. The two wider points are in-cuts on either side of a vert stack, and the two narrower points offer angles for deep cuts. (Most in-cuts angle towards a sideline, while good deep cuts angle towards the middle.)

4x   2x

    1x   3x   (note: not to scale)

Start at one of the deep-cut cones (labeled 1) and make a hard in-cut to cone 2. Immediately change direction and make a deep cut to cone 3, change direction again and make an in-cut to cone 4 in the opposite lane. Change direction again and go deep… rinse, repeat.

So what are you building here?

CUTTING HARD AS A HABIT.

For most players, there is a big difference between track speed and game speed. Pick any game film and watch cutters cruising through their cuts at 80% to see what I mean. This drill allows you to replicate cuts in a game-like environment (cleats, a field, proportional sprints and turns) but under track conditions (no disc, defender or teammates to worry about). Practice bringing your track speed to a game. Make it a habit.

CONDITIONING

This is obvious, but running game cuts at track speed will make you tired. Again, this drill is an opportunity to practice game movements under track conditions. You can practice cutting and still feel, accept, and push through levels of exhaustion that are only achievable under track conditions. Lombardi said it best, 'fatigue makes cowards of us all.'

DECISIVENESS

As a cutter, there are a small handful of situations where your next move is basically scripted. The most common of these is integrated into this pattern: If you were cutting under and you don't get the disc, go deep. If you were going deep and you don't get the disc, cut under.

This isn't news for anyone who's played ultimate for more than a year. While it sounds simple, it's much harder in practice. When a cut expires, young players are often hesitant to immediately cut the other direction without first surveying the field, figuring out where the space is, where the disc is going, what their defender's doing, is it really worth running again when you're kind of tired, etc. Ultimate is distracting. So many decisions!

As a cutter, you can gain an enormous advantage on your defender by making this simple move with immediacy and 100% commitment. When you don't get the disc, immediately stop as fast as you can and go the other way, with track speed instead of game speed. Don't worry about the other stuff – you know this is what you should do, so DO IT. (You can change your cut in a moment if you really need to.) The best part is, your defender is subject to the same decision-making mess I described earlier. They are likely unprepared to defend any cut that sudden and that hard.

This is not easy. Your brain doesn't want to leap before it looks, especially if it's tired. You have to practice this kind of sudden, decisive commitment and make it a habit.

~

Now… that's all great, and will probably help a player of any level to some degree but it's the tip of the iceberg. The true utility of a cutting tree is as an aid to visualization.

Once you've run the tree for a while and you've got the hang of it, start to envision the game around you. The first step to envisioning the game is cutting with your head up. (You can't envision what you can't see.) As you come out of your breaks, get your head up to see what you're cutting towards. Start by imagining a clear lane, and as you get more comfortable you can imagine other cutters clearing from or entering your lane. Once you've taken a few steps, turn your attention towards the disc. This is easy if you're cutting under – if you're cutting deep, see if you can keep your track speed while looking over your shoulder.

Now that you've got your head up, you can visualize the game around you. You're cutting really fast and decisively, but why? What are you reacting to? Did your thrower pump-fake you, or look you off? Did they throw the disc elsewhere? Is your cut too early, or too late? (If you're new to this kind of visualization, it's totally okay to take some slow reps while you work on it.)

Start thinking about the other players, about situations. Look over your shoulder as you're "cutting deep" and imagine the disc being dumped toward the middle of the field, setting up a swing pass. That's your cue to make an in-cut to that side, and by threatening the deep lane with such conviction you've set up your defender perfectly.

Now, what if it's a timing problem? You've started your in-cut across the field, but imagine that the swing got released late and your cut will be too early. As your visualization of the game around you becomes more rich, you can start to deviate from the cone pattern. If you "see" that your under cut is going to be early, cut back three steps deep before cutting under again. Practice improvising.

The most important parts of this visualization come before you change direction. What imaginary event did you react to? What did you "see" – specifically – that let you know you weren't going to be thrown to, that your cut was early or late, that if you delayed one more second your timing would be perfect? These are the cues that will help you see situations quickly and drive your in-game decision making. Learn what cues you're looking for, what they mean for you and practice recognizing and responding to them.

~

There is tremendous advantage to be had in being the first to recognize and react to a developing situation. Most players have had moments like this, when you realize you can cut back and be open, but your defender still thinks that the throw is coming. Throw on the brakes, and they fly right by. It's the best. Think about doing that over and over again. So good. The challenge is that it's pretty hard to pull this off on your first cut. Some people can, but even the best take a lot of space and setup time.

This is why I believe it's so important for cutters to learn to string cuts together, one after another. The best encapsulation of this concept that I've come across is a term from the Japanese game go, called "sente." It roughly translates as "initiative." In go, a player gains sente by making a threatening move to which the opponent must respond. This gives the first player the freedom to make another threatening move, and another, and another, dictating the game to their opponent who has no choice but to respond to each threat.

It's hard to get open in a game, and impossible to guarantee that you'll get the disc – there are just too many variables. But if you can read a situation and make a well-timed, well-spaced cut with speed and conviction, you've created a threat to which a defender (or the entire defense) must respond. If they respond by committing their resources to stopping the threat, you may not get the disc… but you do have sente. Immediately present your defender with another threat, and another, and another, without allowing time and space to recover, and your success is inevitable. Jog, or delay, or pout, or ignore an obvious cue, and you give your defender the opportunity to adjust and recover the initiative. Build your ability to recognize the cues which require response or adjustment, and respond with track-speed and immediate conviction.

A note on structure and clearing:

Surprise, surprise, all four cutters can't do this at once. I'm partial to offensive systems that employ two activated cutters at any one time. With the other 1-2 cutters in cleared positions, there is plenty of field space for both active cutters to gain and maintain sente on their defenders.

Once active, there are two primary reasons for an active cutter to clear.

1. Exhaustion. If you're tired, let a fresh guy ruin his defender for a while.

2. You lose sente. This can happen when you find yourself grossly out of position relative to the disc and cutting space and you can't offer a viable threat. Or, your defender may read the play and effectively reposition before you can counter-cut. In these cases, it's usually better to clear hard and let someone else initiate from their cleared position.

46
BUILDING SPIRIT

On spirit circles

Published April 2, 2014

This past weekend, NW Challenge wrapped up the first half of the season. Congrats to Ohio State for winning soundly. There's a lot to like about this team: they're big and fast, they compliment their two great throwers with consistent disc skills from the rest of the team and they play their best ultimate against the best teams. Also, congrats to British Columbia for quietly going 6-1; you don't want to sleep on this team. They've gotten steadily better over the course of the season and their strength lies in their system. They aren't just relying on Mira to do all the work for them, so when she does it's from a really strong base.

I've strayed from my real goal, which was to talk about the Spirit circles that followed every game. After the Carleton accident, Kyle Weisbrod and I were talking about doing something for Syzygy and his idea was to build on the incredible sense of community that followed the accident by doing Spirit circles. I was enthusiastic, but a bit unsure. I haven't done Spirit circles since Worlds in 2002; I'm not sure how much experience there was from the players themselves. Some of the players had done them with U-23 and U-19, but the general vibe I got was one of uncertainty – what exactly are Spirit circles for?

The general US view on Spirit circles is that they, like song-cheers, are a relic of the hippy-dippy dawning of ultimate and have no practical use in modern ultimate. There was a certain amount of that at NWC – teams often ended by playing reindeer games like Wa! or Look Up Look Down. We (Oregon) played some reindeer games, but we also tried something different – we tried to use the circles as a way to have real and meaningful conversations with the other team. Our first game was against Carleton and even though we had a lot of important stuff to say to them about the accident and about our finals from last year, we flubbed the whole thing and really said nothing. After that we decided that if we were going to screw up in the Spirit circle at least we'd go strong. Then they got much, much better.

Spirit of the Game needs tending; it won't take care of itself without work. Spirit circles can be a useful tool for doing that work. Even at their most hippy-dippy, they build relationships between teams. They provide a forum for meaningful dialogue about SotG and the tone of the game just played. They hold teams accountable to their opponents – teams that end up walking down the dark road often do so in isolation – it is much harder to be a jerk when you have to stand arm-in-arm and talk afterwards.

Here are my suggestions for making Spirit circles a useful tool:

• Go strong. If there is something to be said, say it. Oregon played a game that was quite chippy in the early going because of some weird call situations that came up. We talked about it in the Spirit circle, even though it is uncomfortable to do so.

• Decide who is going to do the talking for your team. It doesn't have to be a captain, but it should be someone who is thoughtful and eloquent.

• Discuss briefly before the circle what you want to say and what you think the relevant issues are.

• Not every Spirit circle is going to be a crazy intense conversation about Spirit. That's good. SotG works just fine 99% of the games that are played, so 99% of the Spirit circles will be pretty bland. These are often the most awkward.

• Tournament directors need to build the time into the schedule for these to happen.

• Washington, Oregon and British Columbia pledged to continue doing Spirit circles the rest of the season; I hope the other teams from NWC continue as well. I'm not exactly sure how this will work or what it will look like, but I am confident that it is good and useful work.

47

INCHES ALL AROUND US

On not missing opportunities

Published April 16, 2014

I watched some men's ultimate this past weekend at Cascadia Conferences. I was surprised by how many blocks they left on the field, particularly on deep throws. I started thinking about why this would happen – the games I was watching were intense, the players motivated and athletic. The first thing I reminded myself of is that defense is actually harder to learn than offense. You can be okay on defense pretty quickly if you are motivated and athletic, but to be great takes learning how to react to a million different little situations. The college men's division as a whole is a great example of this because the offenses are developed and sophisticated beyond where the defenses are.

Once players transition into club ultimate, the defenses begin to catch up. I don't think the defenders this past weekend even knew that the block was a possibility – they couldn't see where or how to get it. I was also reminded of the importance of the nitro, as each of these missed blocks required closing a one- or two-step gap over the last twenty steps before catch. Like all athletic ability, nitro can be trained for and improved, but it's not just speed. Most deep cuts begin at 90%; if you recognize a step early and go to 100% there, you've made up ground. Most deep cuts curve in response to the disc; out-read the offense and take the straight line and you've made up ground. I'd highly recommend it as a skill for defenders, particularly if you cover cutters a lot.

~

I was also reminded this past week of how much one little thing can tip an entire system. We were running a defensive drill at practice recently and it wasn't working quite right. It wasn't effort or focus or understanding. It just wasn't working right. When this kind of thing happens, I usually quit giving feedback for a bit and just watch, trying to see and not look. After a bit I thought it was where our eyes were, so I stopped the drill and told the where their eyes should be. That still didn't work. Eyes weren't in the right place, but why? Then it came to me – our hips were turned wrong. Discussed briefly, adjusted, fixed. Drill runs smoothly.

It is so often the case with the things we are trying to do in ultimate are susceptible to one small change. This is true of drills, pull plays, zones, marking, team culture…everything. The challenge is finding that one thing. It's partly experience, but it's also process. The trick is to see without looking – looking blinds you to everything you aren't looking for. If you aren't sure what's wrong, you often have to let things run wrong while you observe. The change you are looking for is small, simple, easily enacted and flips things over a tipping point.

48
HOW TO CHEAT TO WIN

On cheating

Published May 7, 2014

There is sportsmanship, which in our little sport is embodied in Spirit of the Game, and then there is gamesmanship. Sportsmanship is the ideal of playing within the rules (and the customary understanding of them) because it is the right thing to do. It is concern and respect for your opponent. Gamesmanship is looking at the rules in a lawyerly way, analyzing them and finding opportunities to exploit them. It is looking at the customary ways rules are enforced and tweaking them to advantage. It is always looking to see rules enforced to one's own advantage, rather than impartially, evenly and fairly.

Ultimate's system of self-officiating opens huge doors to gamesmanship that are not open in other sports. It also creates a moral dilemma for teams and individuals. In the NFL, when a coach calls a last minute timeout to ice a kicker it is considered good strategy. In ultimate, if you call a double time-out to throw off another team's rhythm, you're an asshole.

After the debacle of the CUT-Florida final last spring, I had a long conversation with Scoops (Greg Connelly) about SofG. One of his observations (which I agreed with) was that SotG was stronger in club ultimate than college. (Note: this is only true of Men's. Women's ultimate has a strong and thriving sense of SotG at all levels.) This is odd, because the level of gamesmanship is so much higher in club than college. Those crafty vets know all the moves – shouldn't that make their SotG worse? SotG is an agreement between the players and the teams; an agreement of what is and isn't accepted. (This is why behavior that is perfectly acceptable at College Nationals is taboo at city league.) At the Club level, there is widespread agreement that gamesmanship is part of ultimate and, therefore, ok. If I was dumb enough to be marking tight on stalling 7, I knew I had to accept the bullshit pivot-foul-call from the thrower. I knew if I tried to go up line on a Monkey, they'd try to knock me down. But as they say, "If it's in the game…" Contrastingly, in college ultimate, there's no consensus on what should and shouldn't be ok and everyone takes it way too seriously.

This series of articles is my attempt to help with that problem a little bit. My hope is that by understanding the particular techniques of gamesmanship, they will be less effective and that people will have a bit more perspective about them.

49
CHEAT TO WIN: DRAMA

On creating a distraction

Published May 14, 2014

The 2010 CUT-Florida final featured a lot of huge throws, huge Ds, a million calls and a boatload of drama. I don't mean the drama of a thrilling finish (98 Syzygy-Stanford) or a star playing through incredible injury to try to lead his team to victory (92 Cornell-Oregon.) I mean the squalid, petty little drama of 8th graders. Foolishly, CUT tried to use drama against Florida by ratcheting up the physical play on the mark, calling a zillion travels and arguing,

arguing, arguing. Foolishly, because if there is one thing Florida has truly dominated the last few years of college ultimate, it's been the drama department. Why was drama effective for Florida? Why did it help them more than CUT? How do teams use and implement drama?

A LITTLE HISTORY

The first team I ever witnessed win with drama was the three-headed troglodyte of the Seamen, the Irates and Seaweed. In 92, I traveled to Wilmington to play Easterns with CUT and the scene was ridiculous. A bunch of old guys pulled their rusty old trucks up to the fields and stood around smoking cigarettes and laying on the horn for every UNCW score. A pack of ugly, mangy dogs swirled around the trucks and the sidelines snarling, fighting, stealing food and barking, barking, barking. By the time other teams got on the field, they didn't know what to think. Then the Seamen began their brutal fouling on the mark regimen: pushing, bumping and arm-wrapping. If you had the presence of mind to call a foul, it was contested with a sneer – every time. Clueless little college kids were turning over passes left and right only to get their asses skied on the fast break huck. Every goal was followed up by rushing the field, spiking, showing and shit-talking. And this was when any spike was considered unspirited and no one had seen rushing the field except maybe on a game winner.

UNCW lost that year, but they won in 93 and then Gerics exported the game plan to win again with the Irates in 94 (which featured the classic chant "foul-travel-pick…suck my dick" from the disgruntled LPC and UCSB men and ECU's Nat shaking his junk at the crowd after the game) and 95 (which featured Gerics head butting Karlinsky) and in 96 as coach of Seaweed (which featured a lot of verbal abuse and Andre getting chucked in a drainage ditch by the UNCW men.)

But lest you think Toad and Mike made this show up, you have to back up to the granddaddy of all drama creators, NYNY. This mess (and particularly the Hall of Fame aftermath) has been pretty well documented on Kenny's blog and Jim's blog, so I won't go into it too much.

Even before NYNY, there were the originators of bad-boy ultimate, Windy City. There is an (apocryphal) story about their dominating 1986 championship. After they won, destroying all comers, they were reveling and partying with the beautiful, all-glass UPA Championship trophy. Some woman came up and began hectoring them about being unspirited cheaters who didn't deserve to win. What did Windy do? Spiked the trophy, shattering it into a thousand pieces.

Part of what has amused and exasperated me about Florida's antics over the last few years is the histrionic Chicken-Little approach people have taken to this team when their tactics are as old as ultimate. What is different about ultimate and what makes drama especially effective in an ultimate setting is the naivete and innocence that comes with SotG. SotG explicitly states that players will hold respect for opponents above all else and so people are unprepared, offended, angered and intimidated by drama.

It isn't just ultimate where athletes use drama. A few years ago, I went to the opening day of the US Open in New York. Cooter, Carrie and I wandered through the crowds and watched bits and pieces of lots of '[matches, but the one that stands out was between then #10 Tommy Haas, a power-serving giant and an unseeded little Swedish water bug. The Swedish kid was giving Tommy everything he could handle. He was running and scrapping and clawing and exhorting himself and just on sheer energy overwhelming the slow and sluggish looking Haas. He took the first set and was up in the second when Haas threw a fit. It started on the pretext of a botched line call and then carried over into a general rant about the tournament, the organizers and best of all, the music. The match was on one of the smaller courts and classical music was spilling over from a food-court plaza next door. At the height of his fit, Tommy roared, "What is this? The Titanic? I'm not here to listen to music!" About thirty minutes later, it was game-set-match, Haas easily.

THE EFFECT OF DRAMA

The biggest advantage drama confers is mental. Drama has no effect on how fast you are or how well you can throw. It doesn't help you jump higher or mark better. However, it can have a huge effect on the mental preparation and focus of each team.

First of all, when a team uses drama, it gets their opponent thinking about something other than the game at hand. Any time your opponent is focusing on something other than play, they are at a disadvantage. In the 97 Worlds Final, Sockeye was preparing to play Double Happiness. They wanted observers because they were afraid of our call game. (With some justification.) Because it was WFDF, observers were not mandated and had to be agreed upon. Jonny G refused to have observers, not because he thought it'd make a big difference, but because he knew that Double would get all torqued up about us refusing them. The thirty minutes prior to the game featured Jonny in a screaming match with the Double guys while we prepared. We were ready. They were thinking about observers.

Secondly, it puts teams and players in or out of their comfort zone. If you have a high-drama team, I can guarantee they are high-drama all the time: games and practice. They become comfortable playing in a high-drama environment. When they pull their drama hi-jinks in a game, they are unfazed by it, but their opponent is thrown. When Carleton tried to use drama on Florida, they were just chucking the rabbit into the brier-patch.

Drama confers a strategic advantage to teams that want to play slow. Carleton was playing 19 guys and Florida was playing 9. Every stoppage gave Brodie and his boys a chance to rest and catch their breath. The longer the stoppage and the more drama – the more rest. This, too, is an old trick. Schwa 2.0 (winners of 3 silvers: 2 Natties and a Worlds) was masterful at this technique, interspersing exasperatingly long breaks between points with Satterfield-led arguments and tantrums. The effect was to help a Schwa team that ran 10-12 players hang with the much deeper Riot/Verge, Fury and Godiva.

Lastly, if a team has a rep as high-drama, they don't have to do much to be effective at it. Florida, the old North Carolina teams, Sockeye 1.0, Lawn Party didn't have to do much on the field because their prior on- and off-field antics had already done their work for them. People came into those games intimidated and rattled in anticipation of drama that mighthappen.

HOW TO MAKE DRAMA

The best and easiest way is to be an asshole. It's not whether you call foul, but how you call it. Let every infraction of the other team be the worst thing you've ever seen and stoically ignore any complaints about your own behavior. If you can manage to lace your words and actions with disrespect and superiority, all the better.

Cheat. Nothing creates drama like some bad calls. Make them, particularly at crucial points in the game. Not only will this help in the short term, but in the long term it will establish your reputation and people will be thinking about your calls instead of your play.

Make lots and lots of one-sided calls. They don't have to be bad calls (I'll talk about this more next post,) but use them to consistently help your side.

HOW TO BEAT DRAMA

The best strategy is not to participate. When a team wants to play that drama game, let them. By themselves. It's hard to stir up really big drama without a reaction from the other team. Part of the reason it is so much harder to stir up drama at the Club level is that teams and players just shrug it off. At 96 Nationals, Gerics (then with Port City) spit on two Sockeye guys in separate incidents. The second almost initiated a brawl and a timeout followed quickly. Amazingly, wisdom came out of the huddle and we said, "Let's beat 'em and leave 'em." We did, 15-13, and that was the end of their season (and team.)

Don't start it. If you are playing a high-drama team, don't get them rolling. It is tempting as hell, when a high-drama, high-call team starts pulling their same-old-shit to lay into them and let them know what you think. Don't give in. If you do, you are putting them right into their Happy Place.

Know and understand your team's philosophy and stick to it, no matter what the other team does. Although drama isn't really an issue in college women's ultimate right now, this is the strategy we used at U of O this year and I talked about it extensively in this post.

Get observers if you can, but don't make a big deal about it. Don't depend on the observers to do your job for you and don't let them change your team philosophy. (By the way, if you find that teams are always requesting observers against you, you might want to look closely at your actions.)

Channel your anger. You will react to drama. It's human nature to get amped up in those situations, so take that visceral, brain-stem reaction and bring it out in your play.

Laugh at it. Drama lives on being taken seriously and can't handle being laughed at and made fun of. It's hard to do this in a game, but easy to do outside of a game. Peer pressure and respect are huge motivators in our little game, so use them when you can to help push positive change. Be careful, though. It's a fine line between humor and hate. Should you fall on the wrong side of that line, you are making drama yourself.

50

CHEAT TO WIN: THE TICKY TACK FOUL CALL

On calling questionable fouls

Published May 21, 2014

Hey defenders? Ever have that frustrating experience of completely sewing a team up, only to get to stalling 8 and having the thrower call a foul because you brushed their shoulder? Then, when the disc comes back in (at stalling 5), the thrower has had a chance to breathe and reassess the situation and they get off the easy dump? You've just been jobbed by the ticky-tack foul call.

Throwers, here's how you make it happen:

1. Don't call a foul before 6. Ever. If you do, you are doing the defense a huge favor. You are stopping play during the most fruitful period of the stall count when you are most likely to throw a pass for advantage, as opposed to a pass to reset.

2. When you know you are in trouble, pivot. There has been a lot of blog-blather about useless pivoting and it is all true, but this is useful pivoting (even though you aren't going to throw it. Make sure you step forward on your pivot and bring the disc across your stomach as you do so. Both these things will help insure contact, which you need to call the foul. (Bonus: drop the disc when it hits the marker's stomach. Call strip. Watch marker apologetically pick up the disc.) If you get any contact, call the foul.

3. Don't forget the "fast-count" call. If by some miracle (see below) the marker manages to avoid the contact, you can always call a fast count. Everyone breaks this rule (put a clock on it, if you're curious) with most stall counts running about 7 seconds. Typically, people don't call fast count until the count gets down into the 5 second range. This will buy you at least a couple of seconds and if the defender botches the go-back-two rule, call it again and get a full reset to zero. A warning though: this is a weak-ass move and will make you no friends.

How do you stop it?

1. Don't foul. It is the rule after all. It is a huge disadvantage if you mark to ensure that you will never commit a marking foul, though. The only way to do that is to never pressure the thrower, which is an obvious recipe for disaster. A good distinction is between trying to make a play and trying to make a foul. If you get someone on the arm after going for the block, oh well, it

happens. If you get someone on the arm because you're beat and you hold them…well, you're a cheater and you deserve all the ticky-tack foul calls against you.

2. Definitely don't foul after 6 in the stall count. Really, you don't even want to touch the thrower after stalling 6. Smart markers play tight early and loose late. There is some really nice footage of this technique from the Worlds Final. Here is the entire game piece-by-piece, but look at this aerial footage first. Notice Sockeye's (white) hand-checking on the mark early in the count and their dropping off after a count or two. (Interestingly, Revolver plays fairly soft on the mark, instead relying on their down-field footspeed.)

3. Be ready for the jump-back. Most ticky-tack foul calls come from the pivot from forehand to backhand. It is much easier to draw a foul on the backhand side because you can lead with your shoulder and elbow; on the flick-side, you have to hold your shoulder back making it harder to create contact. As you lean in to pressure the flick, be prepared to leap back like crazy when the thrower pivots to the backhand side. I've actually seen throwers fall over when they didn't get the expected contact.

4. Understand that it's all the game. More than any other aspect of ultimate, marking and throwing has challenged the gray area in the rules. Markers press, throwers react, markers react back and on and on and on…I can't tell you how many times I've screamed in frustration at a stalling 7 foul call; not frustration at the thrower, but frustration with myself for giving the thrower the opportunity to call the foul. If you are going to mark aggressively (and you should, it makes for good, physical, athletic ultimate) you have to live with the foul calls.

51
CHEAT TO WIN: MARKING

On tactical marking

Published May 28, 2014

In the fall of 1994, I went to Chicago to play the first ever Tune-Up with Buddha (who became Sub-Zero in 1998.) For a period of five to six years, Tune-Up was the premier preseason club tournament; it was my first experience playing the likes of DoG, Rhino, Chain and Ring. I was arrogant and naive, over-confident and inexperienced. In short, I was about to get my ass handed to me.

There are two moments that stand out from that weekend. About four losses into Saturday, we were playing against Huntsville. I had a pretty good step-around backhand and all day I'd been trying to get it off, only to get hammered by the marker. Finally, frustrated and indignant, I went up to tall Donovan and whined, "You guys are such big cheaters. Every time I try to pivot and throw my backhand, you guys foul me. This doesn't happen in college ultimate. Why can't you play spirited like college ultimate?" Donovan looked down at me and said, "Go back to college," and walked off.

The second was in the DoG-Rhino final: Rick Melner (#00) v. Cork (picture not available). Cork catches the comeback about fifteen yards out and leans out into his classic straight-leg forehand. Ricky climbs right up Cork's leg like they're dancing the tango. It's such a brutal straddle that Cork's pivot foot must have been a good foot-and-a-half behind Ricky. But Cork leans out a little more, throws the goal and calls "Foul," just as cool as a cucumber.

The title of this series is How to Cheat to Win (without Cheating), but we need to be honest: these marking tricks are cheating. They all amount to trying to get away with whatever you possibly can. They depend on putting the onus for legal play on the calls of the thrower, not where it belongs, which is on the play of the marker. Here's how it works:

1. Get away with whatever you can. If you can hug them for ten seconds, do it. If you can fast count them, do it. If you can put both of your arms straight out and keep them from pivoting, do it. Straddle? Check. Less than a disc space? Check. In everyone of these scenarios, you put the thrower in a position to enforce fair play. If they don't, because they don't want to or don't know how or haven't realized you're cheating – big advantage. At the college level, the two most effective tactics are the hug-a-mark (arms straight forward to prevent pivoting) and the not-a-disc-space

mark. That's because college players don't realize what is happening or have the skill set to take advantage of it. At the club level, it's the backpack, the bump on the catch, rough play early in the count. That's because even if the thrower does something about it (like call a foul), it still helps the defense.

2. Even against good throwers, foul between 0-5 in the stall count. It's during 0-5 that throwers do good things like throw goals and big gainers. Stopping play here is a big advantage for the defense, so even if the thrower calls the foul, it's a win for the defense.

3. Backpack. Even if they catch it, they still have to stagger ten steps, losing yardage and time the whole way.

4. Fast count. The advantages here are obvious. On a side note, all of these strategies are designed to induce the rush state in the thrower and nothing hits the panic button like a quick trip to stalling 6.

5. Don't foul between 7 – 10. This is when turnovers happen. Really, it should be rephrased, don't get called for a foul between 7 and 10. See rule #1 for details.

How do you beat it?

1. Poise. The best weapon you have against a hack is the same calm composure Cork showed while throwing that goal. The effectiveness of the fouling mark is partly because of what it prevents you from doing, but even more so because of what it makes you think you can't do. Recognition of the problem is the first step to solving it. Once you realized you are being hacked, you have a number of excellent options.

2. Take the free throw. If the marker is continuously fouling you,

step through and throw the backhand. Call foul. Make sure your move maintains contact with the marker the whole way, so when they try to argue the foul was before the throw, they'll be wrong.

3. Play through. Generally, stoppages benefit the defense. They can rest, assess the situation and stop the rhythm of the offense. The one time a stoppage benefits the offense is if you are about to get stalled. If you are being fouled, then this previous post applies.

4. Play fast. If you are throwing quickly and playing in an uptempo offense, there are far fewer static marking situations. It is the static situations that really allow the marker to clamp down. If you are releasing on stalling 1, before the marker can even get to you, they can't foul you.

5. Observers aren't that helpful for dealing with marking. Well, they are if your team really doesn't know how to deal with physical marks. But for everyone else, the more effective solution is to deal with it yourself in the ways described here. Club Nationals is the proof of this: tons of observed games and physical marking remains endemic.

6. Advocate for the "contact" call. This new call, where a fouled thrower can call "contact," thereby resetting the stall count without stopping play, is a good cure for this problem. It removes the two biggest advantages the defense has in this situation: the opportunity to stop a throw and stop the rhythm of the offense. I talked to USAU Observer Scoops about it over the summer and I know it was in a trial phase then, but I haven't heard much since then. It remains to be seen how the game will evolve around such a big rule change, but I think it will be largely positive. (Although likely requiring another adjustment that will benefit the defense, like stalling 7.)

52
CHEAT TO WIN: THE LIGHTNING ROD

On assholes

Published June 4, 2014

You know the guy, probably before you ever even play his team. "He's sick," your teammates tell you, "but what a dick!" Then you get in the game and he's not that bad…until it's 12-12. Then all of a sudden, he calls three travels, screams at your best defender to "quit hacking me!," spikes it on your star rookie…and smirks his way to a 12-15 victory as your team melts away.

All of the things I've discussed in the Cheat to Win series: drama, traveling, fouls, marking, and all the little gamesmanship moves—they're actually quite difficult to pull off. Like any other aspect of sport, they require a certain level of talent, a certain way of seeing the game, and certainly a flexible sense of morality. Not everyone on your team can or should huck. Not everyone on your team is a great receiver. That's as it should be. Just as strategic aspects of a game plan are divided up, so to are the Cheat to Win aspects. On most teams, this burden is carried by the Lightning Rod.

1. **THE LIGHTNING ROD IS ALWAYS ONE OF THE BEST PLAYERS ON THEIR TEAM.** Creating drama, making tons of calls, stomping around and yelling – these are all ways of saying, "I am more important than you. I matter. You don't." When those things happen, it isn't just to the opposing team that the Lightning Rod is imposing their importance, it is on their own team as well. A rookie or bencher just doesn't have the cache to pull this kind of stuff off. Their team wouldn't put up with it in practice, so it never develops as a behavior. This can be a little different for a men's club team, particularly one that is heavily split O and D. You have lightning rod players on the D team who aren't huge stars on the entire team, but that's because you are actually looking at two separate teams.

2. **THE TEAM HAS TO LOOK AWAY.** This is where the morality of ultimate gets really slippery, really quickly. It's easy to condemn bad calls and cheaters and all those Lightning Rods out there, but they have teammates who tacitly condone that behavior. They may not even condone it. They may criticize it behind that player's back and fight about it in practice, but it doesn't matter because they take the wins. I'd encourage you to read this piece by Tully Beatty of Wilmington. Amid all the crap Wilmington ultimate spit out, Tully was always a class act, but he still took the wins. (Sorry to call you out Tully; you got nailed for having the

courage to say what others just think.)

3. **THERE CAN BE MORE THAN ONE.** It's not the Highlander and often you will find a team where different players are doing different aspects of gamesmanship. This is much more true at the club level than the college level. This isn't surprising. Club teams, because of their greater depth of talent and experience, have a wider division of labor than a college team. Gamesmanship is no exception. There are two recent games that illustrate this perfectly: CUT-Florida and Ironside-Revolver. Notice (or remember) how many of the calls involved Brodie Smith (whether he made them or they were made against him.) In the club final, the calls were spread all over and the little bit of drama Crockford tried to start died pretty quickly when he turned it over.

4. **IT'LL GO BOTH WAYS.** I alluded to this a second ago, while discussing the college finals. When you have a Lightning Rod involved, often their mere presence will generate bad behavior from the other team. Of course, since a Lightning Rod is totally comfortable with calls and drama, this only helps him. When Jonny G went up and played with the Monkey after all his bridges were burned in Seattle, we (Sockeye) were relentless about his play, his calls and his behavior – even though they weren't that bad anymore.

So what does this all mean?

1. **GET HIM OUT OF YOUR HEAD.** Seriously. Why are you letting someone whose game you don't respect get into your head? When you are all torqued up about so-and-so and his calls or spikes or whatever, you're not where you should be, which is focused on your play. The best way is to respect his play, be nice, and when he pulls bullshit, stay nice. When you are playing an inferior team and someone on the other team starts pulling drama and making

a lot of calls, what do you do? You mostly ignore it. You shake your head dismissively and you beat them. Later you think, "what an idiot." This should be your attitude in all such games, win or lose.

2. **CHECK YOUR OWN BEHAVIOR.** Before you whine or criticize too much, make sure you aren't part of the problem. Does your team have crappy, drama-filled games once or twice a tournament? Hm. Do you always have a problem with a particular team? Might be them. Might be the two of you together. Remember, it only takes one or two players to make a team be "a bunch of assholes." You personally might be just fine, but if your captain or fifth-year senior is pulling a bunch of bs...that's on you.

3. **IF YOU REALLY HAVE A PROBLEM WITH A TEAMMATE, VOTE WITH YOUR FEET.** I have seen many players walk off teams because they didn't like the attitude created by one or more players. Usually, it happens in the off-season, but I've seen it happen once or twice midstream. It's bad for the team, but if it's the right decision for you, do it. You can also vote at the ballot box. It's pretty common for the team's biggest criminal to be a captain and captains need to be elected. My on-field behavior was always an issue when we voted for Sockeye captains and ultimately was one of the reasons I quit that job.

53
SPIRIT AT NATIONALS

On the changing world of SoTG

Published June 11, 2014

It wasn't really my intention to rave about Nationals, but once I got rolling it was hard to stop. Sorry; I'll get on track. I skimmed the old rerun Win the Fields that were posted during my Nationals sabbatical and was struck by how different the climate is today from what was going on when I wrote the Cheat to Win series. In 2010, Spirit of the Game was in really bad shape in the Open division in college and the club series was only marginally better. (Like always, women's was in pretty good shape, so the first half of this article will deal solely with the Open division.) I believe that today Spirit of the Game is healthier than it has ever been. Ever.

You have to cast way, way back to find a time were games were less influenced by cheat-to-win tactics and where fewer teams walked away from games filled with resentment. The tone about Spirit of the Game has changed a lot in the last few years; in the run-up to 2010 it was widely believed and professed (particularly in the college ranks) that SotG was a failed system. This is no longer the case.

Spirit of the Game is actually healthier now than it was back at the dawn of the sport because it is no longer reliant on the naiveté and innocence of the participants. College players are so much more experienced, so much wiser, so much more savvy than they've ever been. They are keeping Spirit of the Game healthy with knowledge, not ignorance.

There's no single reason for this shift. Spirit of the Game operates in a pretty complex social setting and it would be very, very surprising if there was a single factor. Instead, there are many possibilities:

- Teams and players are much more experiences. Inexperience makes you vulnerable to cheat-to-win tactics and makes you more likely to overreact to garden variety bad calls.

- People got tired of the bullshit. For two decades, there was always at least one really, really good team that was willing to make a deal with the devil. As bad as dealing with these teams can be, it's almost worse being these teams. Teams built on negativity eventually implode.

- The teams at the top have chosen to play Spirited ultimate. Since the 2010 finals, the very best teams have chosen to minimize call games and drama. These teams set the tone for the sport – we are fortunate that it has been positive.

• NexGen, U-19 and U-23 have made personal connections among the most talented players in college ultimate. It is hard to spend two months on a bus with someone and then be a complete ass when you play them. Spirit of the Game is dependent on relationship between players. Teammates have established relationships that help navigate and diffuse difficult situations.

• The observers have taken a much, much stronger position in the games at Nationals and other high-level tournaments. The 2010 finals was the last time we saw observers sit back and let the game come to them. The subsequent Nationals in Boulder was the beginning of TMFs for cussing and encroachment. The observers began taking a much more interventionist approach; a proactive one that sought to prevent bad situations rather than the traditional reactive style.

~

The Oregon women (who I coach) earned seven TMFs at Nationals – all were on defense. I don't really want to get into a discussion of the merits of the various calls, so I'll just own all seven of them. We earned them. (Good Spirit requires you to be hard on yourself and forgiving of others.) There are a couple larger issues that our situation illuminates – it is these issues I want to draw out.

As far as I know, there were no calls made by offensive players on any of our TMFs. No 'fast count', no 'double team', no 'foul'. In each case, the observer took it upon themselves to make that call. This is reffing and we should acknowledge it as such. This presents a real philosophical and practical dilemma. From the philosophical end, reffing is in direct contradiction to the values of Spirit of the Game. It doesn't matter if they're in orange or in stripes – if they are initiating calls that directly affect play, they are refs. On the practical end of things, reffing takes the decision about how the game should be played out of the hands of the players and places in the grip of a couple individuals. When two teams are in agreement with each other and in disagreement with the observer, weird things happen. I am not so naive as to think that there aren't positives here. Why should a team get an advantage by playing illegally? Shouldn't the observers step in to protect a team from unfair tactics? I thought that the observers were slow to TMF Revolver in last year's final against Sockeye (I know I'm biased); by the time they got around to it, Revolver was sitting on an insurmountable lead. What if they'd 'reffed' the situation instead? Would the Fish be fitting a fourth ring?

Another issue is the vast difference in physicality and aggression between men's and women's ultimate. The Alika Johnston-Dre Fontenot matchup from our quarterfinals against Virginia was spectacular: intense and physical. There was a moment where they got double TMFed for physicality. I watched the observer give the Ts and then looked up and across at the UNC-Wisconsin men's quarterfinal. Two guys were literally shoving each other while a third swooped in to get the D. This was far more physical than what had just happened in our game. No one reacted at all. No blink, no complaint from the sideline, no calls, no TMFs – just business as usual. Men's ultimate is (mostly) happy with the level of physicality in their games. Women's ultimate is (mostly) happy with the level of physicality in their games. They are playing under the same rules. The expectations of what is legal, fair and acceptable are really, really different.

Here is where we start having some real problems. Who decides who's right? Teams? Players? Observers? USAU? What if a team decides to adopt a style of play that is outside the acceptable boundaries? Who decides where these boundaries are? What if a women's team started playing like a men's team? Are they cheating? Under one interpretation of the rules, this kind of play is completely legal, but under another it isn't.

Spirit of the Game is a democratic institution and dependent on the community to maintain it. These issues are not new – for years there have always been discrepancies between what different parts of the ultimate community find acceptable and legal. The rules aren't black and white – they require interpretation to function. The important part is that people talk and discuss, whether chatting privately, over email, in Spirit circles, however.

54
FRAGMENTS

On college nationals

Published June 18, 2014

I keep bugging Deaver, Crawford and USAU about this great idea I have. They keep ignoring me, so hopefully together we can put some pressure on them to make it happen. It is simple: if you win a game at Nationals, you should get to keep the game disc. It doesn't matter if it's the finals or consolation; winning a game at Nationals is a special, special thing. You earned it, your team earned it. And it's only $5 out of their pocket!

~

....that's what ultimate should be. I really don't like stadium finals. We play in a stadium so we can look more legit? We look like we are playing on a borrowed high school football field and that's legit? It feels like I'm wearing my uncle's brown polyester suit to my cousin's wedding – hot, scratchy and uncomfortable. People pay thousands of dollars to sit court-side at NBA games and we're giving that experience up? I say, squeeze it in and surround the game with people. It'd cost about the same to set up rented bleachers behind a couple rows of ground seating. Suddenly the game becomes intimate and loud and enclosed and exciting! You're right there; the players are right there; the play is right there! That's the way.

~

Fragmented fragments....I happened to watch the 'worst' team at Nationals and they were pretty good. The sport has come a long way....I love the pool play format. It is really nicely designed and the asymmetry makes it strategically interesting....it only sucks if your men's/women's team has the same seed....despite all the conversation in last week's post, the observers did an excellent job, particularly since they were understaffed and worked four games a day....I just wish they enjoyed talking trash more....three Midwest Nationals in a row?.... hopefully the Milwaukee fields are by the lake...do you think spiking it out into the lake would be a TMF?

55

RECOVERY

On post-seasons mental growth

Published July 2, 2014

It's a funny time of year for a college ultimate coach. The rest of the frisbee world is moving on and gearing up for Worlds and Nationals, but for me the season is over and everyone has gone home for the summer. There's no practice to plan, no opponents to scout, no tournaments to prepare for. The great industry and mechanic I've built up over the course of the season is still spinning and working, but without any real attachment to a specific process. I find myself going back over film, thinking about process and deep structure. I consider motivation and development. I go back a reread some of my favorite books on coaching. I find new books to read. *The Art of Learning* came in and touched right on this point:

> *Most intelligent NFL players, for example, use the off-season to look at their schemes more abstractly, study tapes, break down aerial views of the field, notice offensive and defensive patterns. Then, during the season, they sometimes fall into tunnel vision, because the routine of constant pain requires every last bit of reserves. I have heard quite a few NFL quarterbacks who had minor injuries and were forced to sit out a game or two, speak of the injury as a valuable opportunity to concentrate on the mental side of their games.*

There is no tunnel vision quite like Nationals. The season slowly and inexorably tightens and narrows until the next day becomes the next game becomes the next moment. This is really one of the glorious elements of Nationals: it is wonderful to have all the other concerns and priorities in life stripped away, if only for a weekend.

I've always marveled at how a player can walk away at the end of a season, not play during the off season and then come back and be better. They haven't played, they haven't watched video or done much of anything and yet they are better. This is the power of recovery. It is also the power of your unconscious mind to work and work and work even when you think it isn't. You cannot pass through an experience like Nationals without improving, even if you never played a point. It looks like those two or three months you spend at home working at the golf course and playing softball with your friends is wasted time, but your unconscious mind isn't wasting any time – it's always working.

You can only completely step away if you have it in you to completely step away. I never really did, but getting out of the day-to-day grind of the season is a chance to work on big picture stuff. It is really nice to have the luxury of not needing an answer – a question can sit partially answered for days, weeks. I can pick it up and roll it around for a bit and then leave it be until later.

This isn't about ultimate, but I am undergoing the simultaneous experience as a teacher. Relieved of the daily burden of papers and lesson plans and meetings and class, I can step back and think about the big picture stuff. Am I emphasizing the things I want to emphasize? The hidden things I am teaching – how to relate to authority, the structure of mathematics, what it means to 'do' math – are these the things I want to teach? How can I get the kids to do what they need to do? How can I get the kids to invest into the work instead of me dragging them to the work? So many of these questions are actually the same questions I am asking about ultimate: Are we the team we want to be? Is the team taking away what I want them to be taking away? Can I even define these things?

~

Club players are in a far different spot. The broad part of their season is over and they are entering the narrow funnel leading to Worlds and then Nationals. They no longer have weeks and months to burn; for them time has become days and moments. In the chapter Searching for the Zone, Waitzkin discusses how to recover in an exceptionally short amount of time. In fact, he identifies rapid recovery as a key element to performance. Successful performers have the ability to rest, rejuvenate and refocus in a very short amount of time. Ultimate, with its built in 90 seconds and O-D splits, is perfect for this type of recovery. Here are some practical suggestions:

1. **THROWING 10S.** This is my rest and refocus tool of choice. As you feel focus slipping or find yourself struggling with a rough patch of playing, grab a partner and throw ten forehands and ten backhands. It is quick, simple and brings you back into your focus rapidly.

2. **MUSIC.** I've always been annoyed by people listening to music while the rest of the team is warming up or between points. I think it is crucial for the team to be connected during this time. Ultimate isn't track or tennis, you are on a team. You have to succeed together and you have to work together – get off your iPod. Strangely, I do think there might be a place for listening to music if you are in struggling place. Did you get benched for a couple points for turnovers? Checking out for a titch might be the right choice.

3. **SIT DOWN BETWEEN POINTS.** This is another odd one to consider, but what about mandating tent and sitting time after playing a point? Again, I think it is crucial that people are up and supporting their team – sidelines obviously play an essential role particularly on defense. But look at team sizes – most are well over twenty. You could easily put seven on the line, seven in the tent and still have plenty to help the defense. I know that one of the rare games I spent in the tent, the 2004 Finals, is also the game I was the most focused and clearheaded throughout. There have also been times with Fugue that we've mandated players stay in the tent because of hot weather and these games turned out fine.

56
A WINDY OPEN

On playing in the wind

Published July 9, 2014

It was lovely to have a steady stream of ultimate on the television this past weekend. There were times I sat and watched intently and there were times I just had it on the in the background; but the simple pleasure of being able to watch ultimate at home is hard to quantify.

The biggest storyline had to be the wind. It all but guaranteed a

Revolver victory and made the women's final into a slug fest. Although it is hard to feel the wind through the monitor, once you know what the conditions are for each game they are an excellent resource to learn how to deal with the wind. Taken as a whole, the catalog of games (both NexGen and ESPN) from this weekend serve as an excellent example of how to game plan for the wind. The games from the first two days were played in mild, but increasing wind. Things started as a thrower's wind* and progressed into moderate upwind-downwind conditions. On the semis and finals days, the wind worsened to the point that routine throws became an adventure. Accordingly, strategy must shift for each circumstance.

The first thing to realize about playing in windy conditions is that wind isn't something to fight against; it is just something else to use. There are throwing possibilities that exist on a windy day that aren't there on a still day. There are defensive possibilities that aren't there on a still day. The relative value of choices (offensive and defensive) changes dramatically. The best way to play the wind is to accept these and adjust accordingly.

As an example, consider marking in an upwind-downwind game. If the offense is going upwind, I want to keep my hands low and do my best to prevent low, flat releases. If the thrower wants to throw high or seriously banked throws, I'll let him – those kind of throws struggle significantly going upwind. Turn things around and I'll put my hands high. The bottom always drops out of downwind throws and I am happy to have a thrower release low in this circumstance.

Two throws stood out to me as making a significant difference on the outcome of games. In the Traffic-Brute Squad semifinal, Brute was able to pull away in the second half by throwing around backhands down the sideline. These were thrown for power and distance; they were anchored by excellent technique with lots of stabilizing rotation. Conversely, Traffic was doomed once they began letting these throws out. (Discipline in a highly windy game is often defensive – you can't afford to make a mistake that leads to a goal.) The second throw was Revolver's gut-throws in the final. Again and again, they ripped forehands right into the receiver's gut at short distance. These throws are fast and powerful, they are minimally susceptible to the swirling wind. The challenge is that they have to be very accurate and the receiver has to handle a bullet at close range. Revolver's use of these throws was exceptional – it displayed impressive tactics and technique.

An interesting paradox of ultimate is that as throwing skills have increased, the percentages of throws that are hucks has decreased. Unthinkingly, you'd expect that as throwers get more skilled, they'd be more accurate on long throws and the number of these would increase. Oddly, there's been a decrease in the amount of hucking in the last ten or so years – a decrease that coincides with broad increases in across-the-board throwing skills. This is connected to the Swing-Pass Fallacy**. Because teams can throw so well up and down their rosters, the chance of an execution error on a swing or underneath pass is very, very small, while the odds of completing a huck haven't gone up as substantially***. Severely windy conditions radically change this math, returning all of us to the days of our first ever forehands. Every throw becomes an adventure and exercise in concentration. Hucking suddenly becomes a really, really, really good choice. At the lower percentage levels of the sport, huck-and-play-d is the best choice. At the upper levels, you get a game exactly like this year's US Open Finals: every huck that has a reasonable chance of success gets thrown.

A sophisticated understanding of the wind game means that you don't always huck. There are moments where you can gain an easy twenty with minimal risk. Although field position is always part of the calculation, the farther you advance down the field, the smaller its importance. Making decisions is a complicated process of calculating expected value over and over again. Obviously you can't sit down during the point and run the numbers. (Even though ten seconds is a loooong time.) It takes a lot of experience to internalize the appropriate decisions for any situation in ultimate – the challenge for the teams at the Open is that very few of them get the opportunity to play in the wind on any kind of regular basis. It shouldn't be a surprise that Sub Zero over performed this weekend – they are the only team that routinely sees the kind of wind conditions that were in effect.

57
THE RULEBREAKER

On breaking the mold

Published July 23, 2014

Every offense has rules, and every team has that one player who can't be convinced to follow them. Despite the immense amount of frustration that these players generate in their teammates, there is often a lot of value in what these players bring. An offense where everyone follows the same rules and does the same things in the same circumstances is often too one-dimensional and too easily shut down by opposing defenses. The rule-breakers in a team offense often provide a necessary degree of unpredictability and multidimensionality. Intelligent teams make allowances for this type of rule breaking; in fact, when properly designed into the offense, rule breaking isn't breaking any rules.

In reviewing the US Open film, I was struck by the similarity between the manner in which Revolver deployed Beau Kittredge and Bravo utilized Jimmy Mickle. Both of them fit into the classic role of the rule-breaking best player; the surprise is to see this happening at the top of elite ultimate. This role has long been a staple in college teams because of the lack of depth at that level. In college, these players typically operate as handlers, and their rule breaking is limited to liberal shot selection, holding the disc and a lot of gimme-the-disc reset cutting. What Kittredge and Mickle are doing is more expansive than classic college version of this job, and importantly, it's designed to be part of their team's strategy.

They are employed as downfield cutters in pull plays. Both players are the featured targets in the 3-spot on a majority of pull plays from their team, with each operating within his team's offensive framework. For Kittredge this means isolation cutting out of the sidestack. Because he is so feared as a deep receiver, he often gets free yards coming under. Bravo organizes space through motion, almost always beginning their plays with a misdirection cut (or two) by a secondary receiver and then working Mickle back into their wake. Because he is so feared as thrower, he is often wide open going deep.

They both can cut whenever they want. Other players on their team are often required to clear into dead space or wait patiently and spread the field, but not these two. They are entitled to cut when and where they want, often bending the shape of the offense to their cuts. As an example, Kittredge often runs full speed for the endzone immediately after releasing the disc. This cut is almost always open (the marker started even with him), but it eats the entire lane from short to deep and its success requires some very intelligent cutting/clearing from the other downfield players.

They provide a pressure valve for their teams. When the stall count gets high and the offense is struggling, both teams turn to Kittredge and Mickle. For Revolver, this usually means hucking it to a not-very-open Kittredge. Bravo's work is more complex, with Mickle often working the early part of the stall count to set up a crease he can exploit between six and eight; a surprisingly high percentage of Mickle's touches come in this part of the stall count. (Defenders typically position themselves to deny the horizontal cut to the open side; this is standard positioning. Mickle will jog set up to get a window above or below the defender and then attack it. Essentially, the crease is created by the defender getting an eighth or quarter step out of position.) One of the things both teams do very well is throw to their receiver; what this means for Revolver is hucks high and far. For Bravo this means soft throws up into lateral space around the disc. There are very few defenders who can manage Mickle's size and quickness under these circumstances.

Both operate away from the disc. This is very different from the classic college approach to this position which holds the rule breaker constantly near the disc. Revolver and Bravo are talented and don't need their best players to handle the disc every second or third pass. Although there are times they do…

Both are often isolated in endzone offense. In this phase of the game they are so similar, each providing a big, athletic target. Where Kittredge uses speed, Mickle has quickness, but the differences are minor.

There are some real differences in the way these two players are employed by their teams. Revolver has a long history of relying on a handful of dominant players to drive their offense; a big part of their clarity of spacing is built around the fifth, sixth and seventh players on any given line spending a lot their time to get out of the way usefully. Within that framework, Kittredge is merely accepting the mantle left to him by Cahill and Watson. So what you see from Revolver is a lot of clarity and a lot of open space. Bravo is working with a very different model. They free everyone up to do everything which is why you see Matzuka going deep so much, Watson and Westbrook doing a little bit of everything…the only consistent o-line guy with a clearly defined role is Roehm. In this anyone can do anything offense, Mickle stands out more for how often they go to him than how he fits.

Their cutting styles are different as well. Kittredge's is simple – he just asks you if you can keep up with him in a straight line. Since you can't, he is open. Mickle's is built more around the jogging or walking set up followed by explosiveness; he works his defender for a little horizontal crease and then attacks it.

I would expect to see more of this kind of offense in the future; the only reason more teams don't use it is because they don't have the top end talent to pull it off. As the talent pool expands, there will be more and more players who can carry this load and more and more teams will choose to put their eggs in one basket. This is how professional sports work; despite huge numbers of talented people, strategy runs ever more strongly through the most talented.

Part of my motivation in thinking about this was wondering about terminology. We can expand our strategic understanding just by naming things; Kittredge and Mickle are doing the same task and once that task is identified it can be simply named. I could have just as easily written this article about the peculiar take on handlers used by Karlinsky and Matzuka or about the role Genevieve LaRoche fills for Fury; they are handlers and cutter, but their roles are defined beyond the basic vanilla elements of those job descriptions and once described, could be named.

58

HELP: PART 1

On helping in man defense

Published July 30, 2014

In ten years, help defense will be the standard technique used by all man-to-man defenses; vanilla, just-cover-your-guy methods will be considered old and out-of-date. Instead, man-help defense will be the vanilla. This is an adjustment that professional sports made long ago. Basketball has honed help defense to a science (1, 2) measured in feet and inches. Soccer defenses are built on outnumbering the offense, and a one-on-one situation is a sign of a significant defensive breakdown. In American football there are maybe three cornerbacks capable of covering the best receivers one-on-one.

Historically, ultimate teams have been able to get away with playing just-cover-your-guy defense for a couple of reasons. First of all, the total talent pool has been pretty small and so there are usually just a couple of teams at the top whose athleticism is far superior to everyone else's. If you're a step faster in every match-up, just-cover-your-guy is really effective. The other reason, also related to the total depth of talent, is that people just aren't that good yet. (I mean that in the nicest way, but we are just entering a period where the best throwers have been throwing from childhood and there are still many great players who didn't start throwing until they were eighteen. Not a recipe for achieving peak skill with a disc.) Defenders are capable of winning one-on-one match ups because throwers haven't reached their full potential. But they are really close to the point where that defensive one-on-one will become unwinnable. There are already several match-ups in elite ultimate that fit that bill.

I want to really clarify what I am talking about here. When I say help-man, I am talking about a defense that is built out of a strict man-to-man with an emphasis on creating temporary double-coverages. Although techniques like poaching and switching are employed here, the general idea is to prevent rather than generate blocks. So in that vein, the strategy Team Japan used against Fury in Sakai (where they consistently sagged off Fury's handlers to clog the center of the field) is a perfect example, but the 2002 Sockeye poach and switch defense is not because it was primarily geared at generating blocks. I'm not talking about defenses like a clam, FSU or Oregon's help-zone, either. I love those defenses, but while they share techniques with help-man, they are fundamentally different because their base structure is zone.

Before we can get into the meat of this, we need some more definitions regarding space. One way to conceive of space on the field is to divide it into active, on-stage, and dead. In a vertical stack, the two alleys are active, the dump, front and back of the stack are on stage and the middle of the stack is dead space. In a horizontal with a centered disc, all six cutters are on stage and it is the space right in front of the disc that is active.

Now that we've laid the groundwork, we can get into the meat of the concept. There are many, many different tactics for help defense that depend on the shape of the offense and the location of the disc, but there are also a few guiding principles that provide a framework for planning these tactics.

THE TWO MOST IMPORTANT FUNDAMENTALS TO BUILD INTO YOUR BASIC DEFENSIVE SKILLS ARE KEEPING YOUR HEAD UP AND COMMUNICATION. These two fundamentals are most important. First, play with your head up. This is a physical action that prepares you to take mental action. Just-cover-your-guy defense requires that you look at your assignment and nothing else. Help-man requires that you know what is going on around you; to do that you need to lift your head. In the still below, you see the three Sockeye defenders in the back of the stack are heads up looking at the whole field. The second fundamental is communication. As a team gets better at playing help defense, switches and helps will happen naturally without any spoken words, but not always and certainly not at the beginning. It doesn't take a lot of talking or a lot of words. The best thing to say is the other defenders name and then point at what you want them to see. If you've sorted out your tactics ahead of time, the switch or help becomes second nature here. It is equally important that all the defenders play with their ears open; nothing is more frustrating that screaming at a teammate who seems to be willfully ignoring you.

If you are covering a player who is in dead space, you should move away from them and help defend the active part of the field. There is no reason to stay right on an offensive player who is in the dead space of the field. All you are doing is allowing clean, open space for the active cutters to work in isolation. You often have to move pretty far to be effective, sometimes as much as 15-20 meters. Well spaced offenses make you choose by moving the dead space cutters a long, long way from the active parts of the field.

YOUR HELP POSITIONING SHOULD ALSO PREPARE YOU TO RETURN TO YOUR ASSIGNMENT AS PLAY DEVELOPS. This isn't zone or junk defense. You have an assignment. It is essential that you help in such a way as to allow you to return to your assignment if necessary. Usually this is after some kind of lateral pass that shifts the angles on the field.

IF YOU ARE IN THE ON-STAGE SPACE, LOOK TO HELP OPPORTUNISTICALLY, BUT STAY HOME. The simplest example of this is last back in a vertical stack. You are covering the person most likely to cut next, so you need to stay with them, but you are also the person best situated to help on deep cuts running down the lanes on the sides of the field. So you do both; stay home and use your fundamentals to put yourself in a situation to help or switch.

PLAY DIFFERENTIAL DEFENSE. This is particularly true for juniors and college teams, but when you are playing a team with a single dominant thrower it often makes more sense not to help off of them. Helping, particularly around the disc, usually means giving up a swing or a dump to prevent a yardage gaining comeback or huck. If all the players on the other team are equally talented, this is always a good choice. Obviously, this isn't the case and when a team has one really great thrower it often pays to deny them the disc whenever possible.

I am going to wrap up for this week and return next week with a close examination of helping in handler sets, where to help in different offensive sets and some specific examples from recent games.

59

HELP: PART 2

On seperation vs commitment

Published July 30, 2014

Welcome to Part 2 of the help defense series. If you are reading this at Worlds I hope you are playing well and having a wonderful time.

At the end of last week's post I promised a look at handler help defense, but as I prepared for and talked to people about this week, I realized I wasn't ready to tackle that issue just yet. What I really need to take care of is some more basic thinking about help defense, particularly in relation to specific offensive structures. So much of playing defense is situational. In fact, once you move beyond the basics of sticking with your assignment, forcing, and some rudimentary footwork, all defense is specifics. How you play in the wind or on a handler or on a taller cutter or with a sidelined disc or with a developing give-and-go…there are so many tiny details to be learned and mastered. Help-man defense isn't any different from any other defensive technique in this regard. Last week we looked at the very first layer of thinking about help-man; this week we'll look at the next layer down. This means taking a look at distinct helps and rotations for specific formations and situations. Just be aware that like all defense, there are a million what-ifs, hypotheticals and possibilities that have to be learned and that this post covers initial guidelines that serve as a foundation for these details.

There is an essential technique and concept that comes up several times in this week's post: the idea of separation vs commitment. Often help defenses are destroyed by way, way, way too much separation. When you think of the over the hill city leaguer who never covers his assignment, this is the player who has allowed too much separation. It is essential that you are able to recover to your assignment should the need arise. The trick here is to play with commitment, but with as minimal separation as possible. As an example, imagine a simple two person in-out split. There is no reason for the backing defender to be ten yards deeper than everyone else. One yard and 100% commitment to covering the out will suffice. Only dropping a single yard also puts the defender in position to recover should the circumstance require it.

Another key technique is recover, switch, or cascade. A recover is when you help briefly and then return to your assignment. A switch is when you trade assignments with another player. A cascade is a series of assignment changes involving multiple defenders where the assignments change sequentially as first one and then another then another problem is addressed. In theory, a cascade could go on and on, but functionally they are a mess if they get beyond four players and it's usually best to have everyone match up cleanly at that point.

VERTICAL

I am going to address side stack later, so vertical here means a well-defined central stack with active spaces on either side of the stack. Typically there will be a single dump, but there are variations with no dump (80s) and two dumps (which isn't very effective, so no one really uses it). In a vertical, the active spaces are on either side of the stack, the on-stage spaces are the front, back and reset parts of the stack and the dead space is the central portion of the stack. (Diagram 1)

Diagram 1: Vertical Spaces

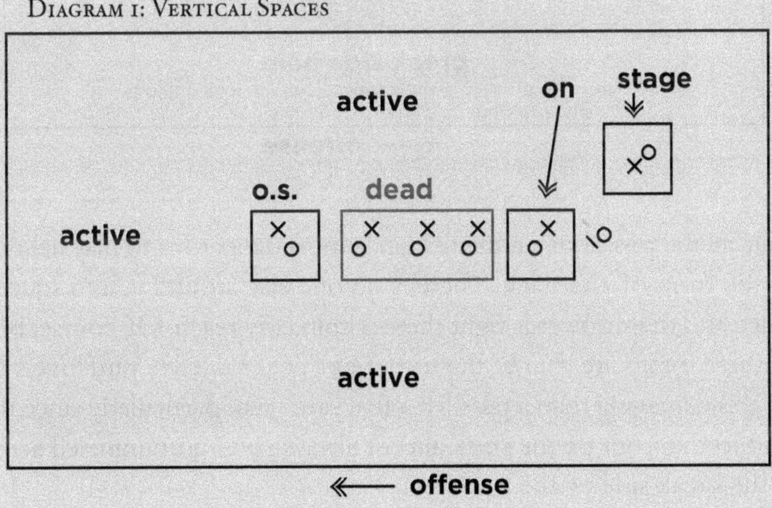

Relying on the foundational principles, the defenders in the dead space should be looking to help. The best method is to have two of the dead space defenders help into each of the two lanes. (Diagram 2) The open side helper should drop 5-10 yards out in to the lane. The break side helper should play right in the middle of the stack with minimal separation but total commitment to defending the break side. These two defenders are looking to help teammates who are actively defending cuts in the lane and simultaneously protecting each other's assignments. Depending on how the offense responds, this could end in any of the three outcomes: recover, switch or cascade. (That's the next layer of detail down.)

Diagram 2: Vertical Help

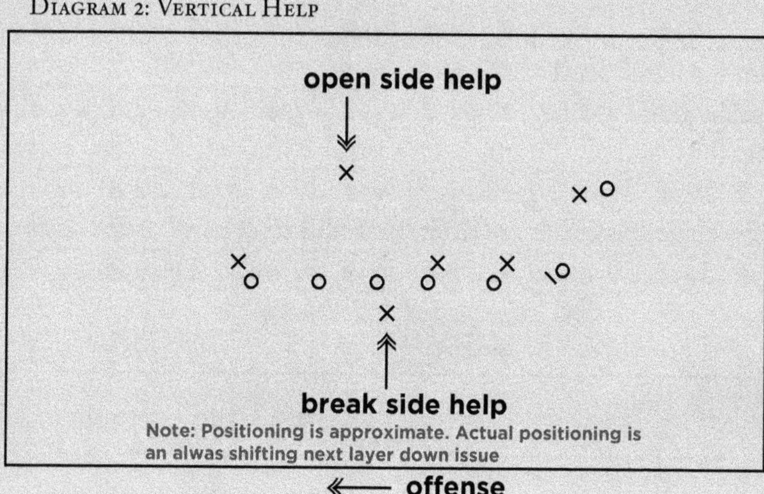

Of all the positions on the field, it is most dangerous to play help off of the front of the stack. There is no one else around you to squeeze space and the thrower is right there within easy reach. Of course, both of these things are true of the reset, but a pass for a five yard loss is far, far less damaging than a pass for a five yard gain, particularly since that shot to the front of the stack almost always gives untrammeled access to the break side of the field.

HORIZONTAL

The strength of the horizontal is that all six of the players are either in active space (the two central cutters) or on-stage (the other four). (Diagram 3) The weakness is that two of those four on stage players, the resets, are in terrible position to threaten much more than a swing to the sideline and the sideline is a great place for the disc if you are the defense.

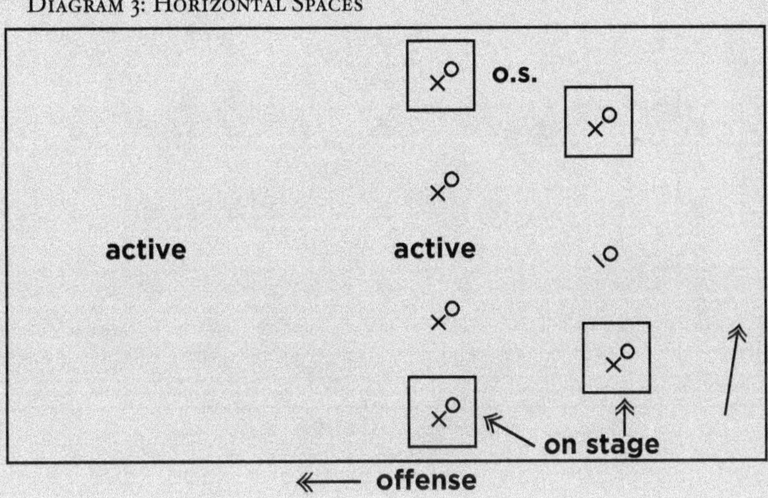

The classic way to play help defense on the horizontal is to leave the handlers, but since I am going to address handler help in detail later on, in this post I'll look at how to help downfield. When the disc is in the center of the field (Diagram 4), the best way to help is to have the two side defenders drop off into deep space to protect the central defenders from the huck. The central defenders play the underneath. The challenge is that there are two throwing lanes coming back to the disc and the single underneath defender often gets split. It is essential that they play the interior lane and leave the outside lane to be squeezed by the handler defender. Alternatively, you can just bring the side defender from the break side, but they have to come a long way to be effective and that much separation often puts too much pressure on the marker to stop a pretty easy break for big yards. Really, the horizontal is very powerful from the middle of the field and you are best served using your help defense to drive the disc to the sideline where the offense will struggle much more.

Diagram 4: Horizontal Help - Centered Disc

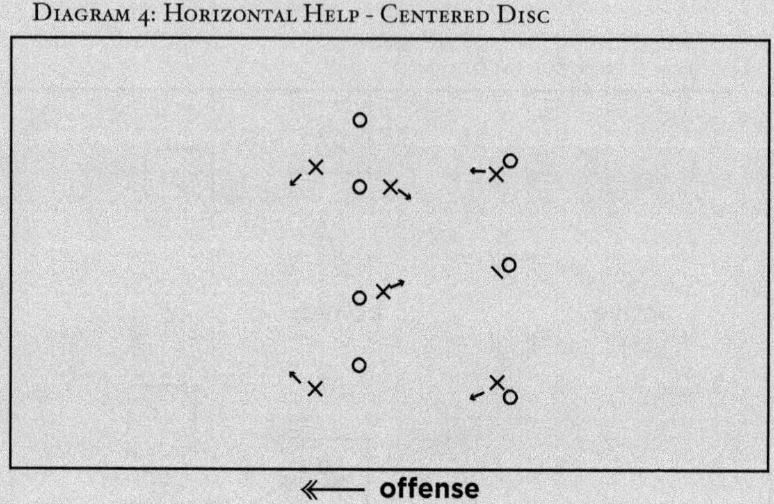

Once you've driven the disc to the sideline, (Diagram 5) the two weakside cutters are horribly positioned and both should be left stranded on the far side of the field. One defender should help deep, the other under. As with the vertical, they should be helping the strongside defenders who are defending active cutters while simultaneously supporting each other.

Diagram 5: Horizontal Help - Sideline Disc

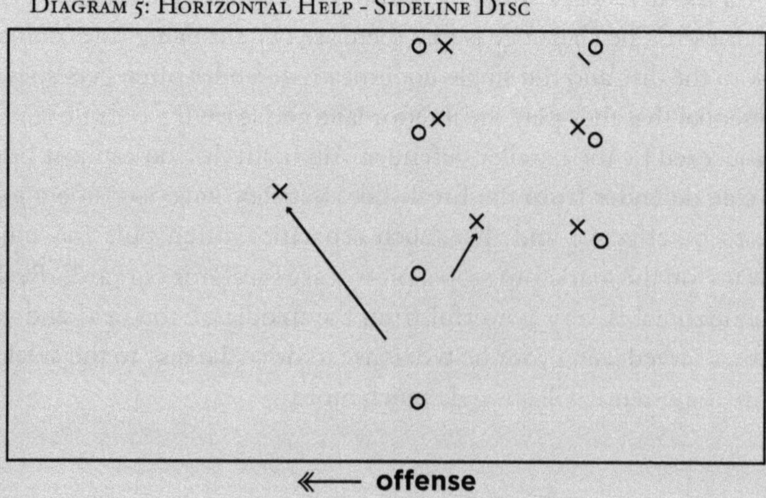

SIDE STACK

There aren't many teams who use this as a flow offense, but lots of teams run this as a pull play. This help system is 99% effective as long as you can live with shuffled match ups. The strength of the side stack is that it creates an ocean of space and the weakness is that it puts a lot of offensive players in some really dead space on the field. The strength is that a help defender is only effective by giving up a huge amount of separation and the weakness is that it is really hard for the offense to take advantage of that separation. (Diagram 6)

DIAGRAM 6: SIDE STACK SPACES

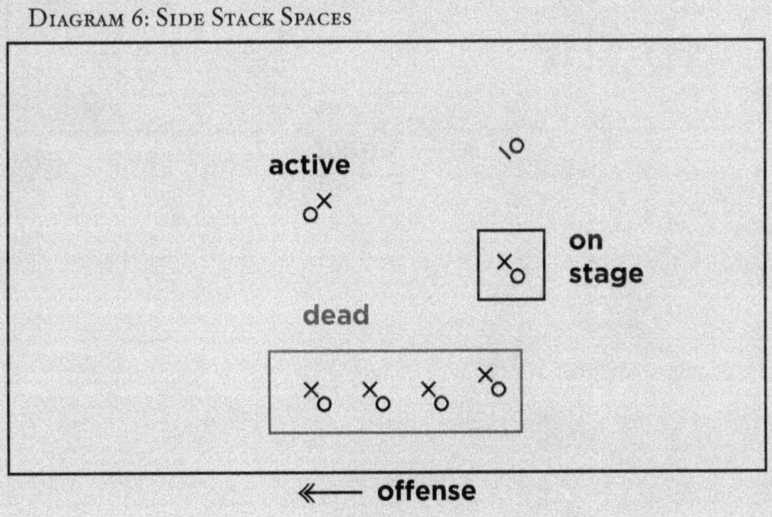

The help (Diagram 7) begins with the deepest defender in the side stack dropping out and playing as a deep-deep, allowing the active defender to front. Effectively they've double-teamed the active cutter. Two other side stack defenders operate very similarly to the help defense in the vertical: one of them drifts out into the lane and protects the central under lane and the other stays with the stack to react as necessary. (They are primarily responsible for containing flood plays and counter flow that are looking to take advantage of the help separation.) This help scenario almost always results in a cascade as the offensive players react and transition into flow.

DIAGRAM 7: SIDE STACK HELP

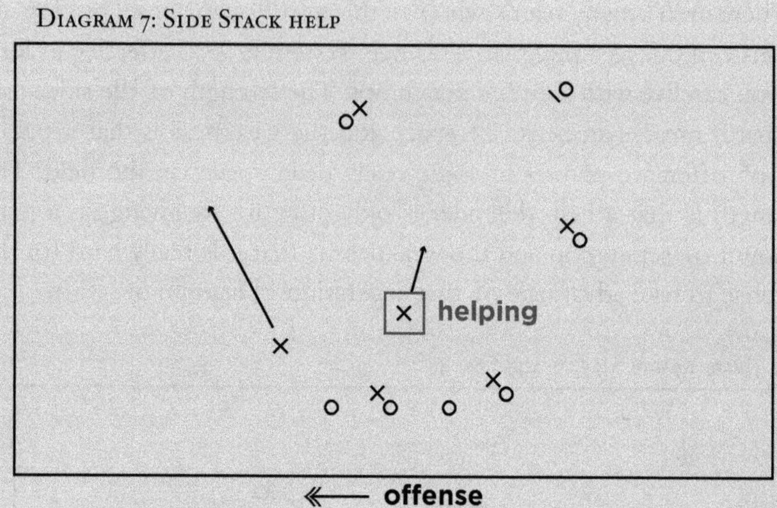

60
HELP: PART 3

On handler help

Published August 13, 2014

In this third installment of the help defense series, I will focus on handler help. For our purposes, handler help will mean playing help defense while covering someone who is even with or behind the disc and in a fairly defined handler position. I will briefly discuss help in flow at the end of the post, but that is really a different idea altogether. Before I start though, I need to clarify a couple of vocabulary points. Handler is a pretty vague term in ultimate because it can refer to a lot of different things depending on the circumstance. For precision, I'll use handler to refer to anyone in the area around the disc including the thrower and reset to refer to those players other than the thrower. Depending on the set, there could be as few as one reset (no dump) or as many as three (German).

The biggest problem you are confronted with while playing handler help is that you are already on stage, so leaving your assignment to help immediately makes him or her open. If you are defending down the field, you rarely want to leave your assignment wide open unless you are getting a block or stopping a goal, but around the disc there are some factors working to make leaving someone wide open a good idea. First, you aren't giving up yards. Because of the positioning of the handler, even if they do get it, they aren't gaining anything. Second and perhaps more importantly is the rhythm of the offense. All offenses have a rhythm to them, they breathe like a person, an expanding and contracting that is connected to both the flow of play and the stall count. Most offenses don't want to throw swings or dumps until higher in the stall count, instead preferring to use the early seconds to look downfield for big yardage gainers. This creates a kind of temporal dead space; although the thrower could go straight to your assignment, they won't and so you are free to help. Specifically, many of the offenses that young and inexperienced teams play require the thrower to look at the dump at a certain moment in the stall count, usually 5 or 6. Look for this, and when you recognize it, take advantage of it to help while simultaneously preparing to recover and play tight defense.

This brings us to a second key concept for handler help, **flash and recover**. Handler defense often puts you within a step or two of the throwing lanes. As you are playing defense on your assignment, keep your head up and when see a developing cut downfield, flash into the lane and then quickly recover back to your defensive positioning. If you are lucky, you will get a block here, but more often you will stop the throw, chop tens of yards off of a comeback cut or give another defender time to close separation.

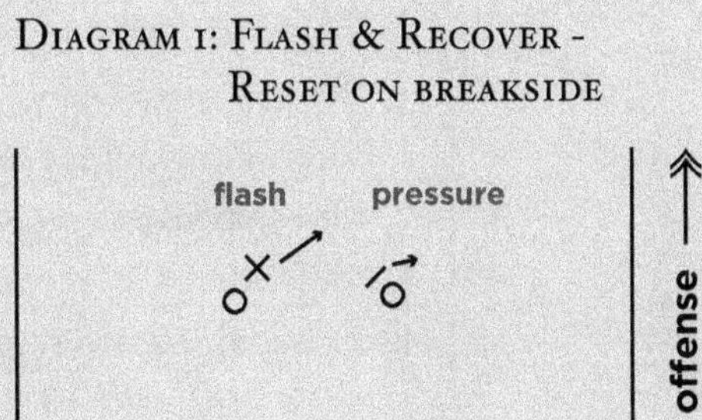

One specific flash and recover technique involves working off of the break side. (Diagram 1) There are many offenses that put the handler reset out on the break side to prevent their defender from helping on the open side. Defenders often oblige the offense because they don't realize who they should be working in tandem with: the marker. As a defender, you are in the around space and so the marker doesn't need to cover it as much. A couple quick words (their name and 'I got around') is all it takes to let a defender who is aware of this stunt know what they need to do. They slide their mark over to shut down the inside out and pressure the open side while you cover the around. When the circumstances dictate that you move (and they will), a simple 'I'm out' lets the marker know to return to standard positioning.

Another very common two person technique is the slide over. Both examples of this technique involve the marker and the handler defender switching assignments.

This is an easy switch once you see it; it is actually more work to stay with your assignment because you have to overrun the other defender. In the first example, (Diagram 2) the offense is attempting to run a give-and-go. The key moment is when the first throw in the give-and-go is released. The defender (B) on the pass can see the give-and-go in development on the release; either the thrower is already at full speed or they are using the more slowly developing up-seal and

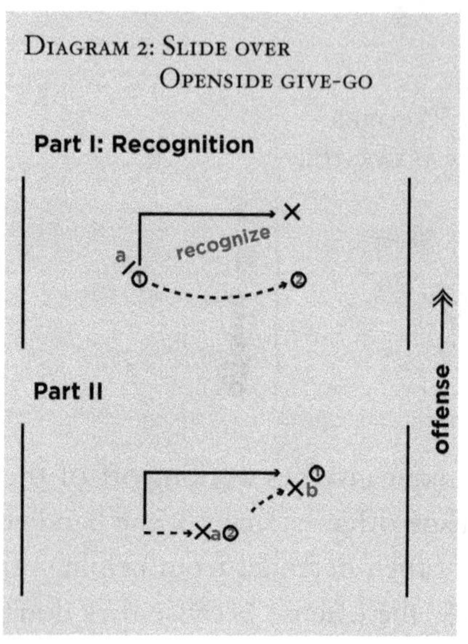

over move (Pictured; it involves taking an initial step or two straight forward, sealing your marker away from open side marking and then attacking across the field.) It doesn't matter which, just that the defender (B) recognizes that the original thrower is coming their way. Instead of moving down and marking, the defender (B) stays about five yards off of the disc and waits – the give-and-go cutter comes right to them and the original marker (A) slides straight over and establishes a second mark in a row. Be aware that there is a brief hole between the two defenders. I'd recommend leaving it barely open because the cost of fully shutting it down is to give too much space around the edges, but that decision is another layer down.

The other example of the slide over (Diagram 3) is off of the dishy reset move.

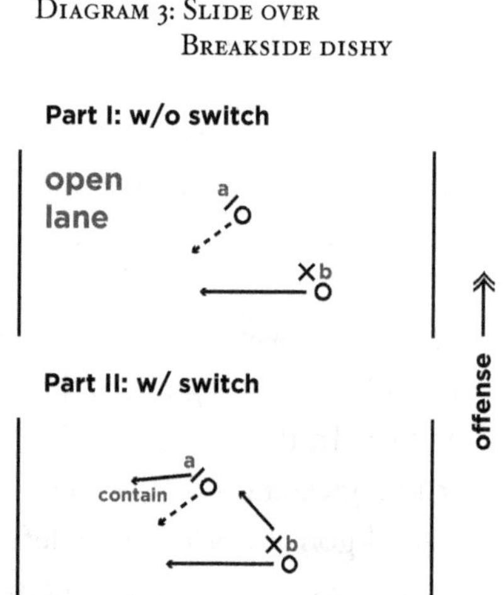

The dishy is where the handler, working entirely behind the disc, runs from the open side to the break side, receiving a little lift pass on the way. With the defender (B) trailing, the dump now has access to the entire break lane. Central Florida's Sunny Harris used this move repeatedly in their semifinals campaign last spring. Although the defensive moves are similar to those used against the give-and-go, the process is in a slightly different order. This time, it is the marker (A) who does the recognition; they can see the dishy cut developing right before their eyes and it is a simple matter to continue their momentum out into the throwing lane to stop the continuation. As with the slide over on the give-and-go, there is a brief gap between the two defenders; it is imperative that the other defender (B) quickly reposition so as not to be exploited.

The next technique I want to look at is off of two-reset sets.

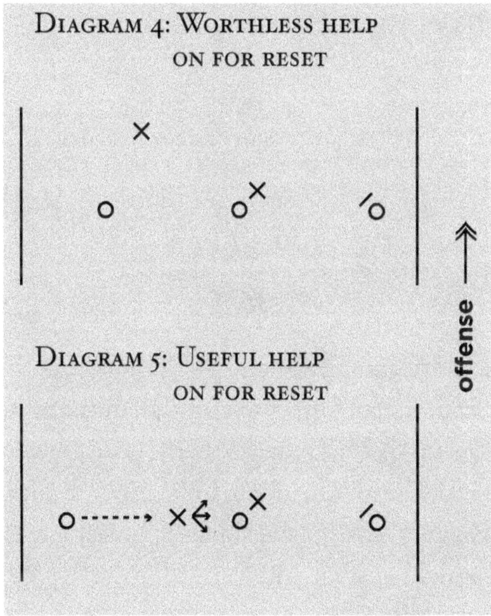

Typically, you'll see these sets as a part of a horizontal offense, but sometimes they show up as a sideline modification to a vertical stack. Let's look first at the case where both resets are on the same side of the disc. In this situation, the far reset defender is in dead space and definitely should be helping. Typically what people do is drop straight back or slightly toward the disc and back, hoping vaguely to protect some of the interior lanes. (Diagram 4) This is the most worthless thing you can do. You are leaving your assignment open, but you aren't really covering anything else. All you've done is moved from dead space on your assignment to dead space separated from your assignment! The best thing to do in this situation is to move straight toward the disc and pressure the reset space. (Diagram 5) Depending on the circumstances, you can be more or less aggressive, but at a minimum you should be driving the reset in to a major loss of yards and then not letting them swing the disc back out again. There are a few rare occasions when it makes sense to drop all the way out into the cutting lanes from here, but be aware that you have to go a long, long way to be effective and that your recovery will be challenging.

Diagram 6: Hanlder Help
Split Resets

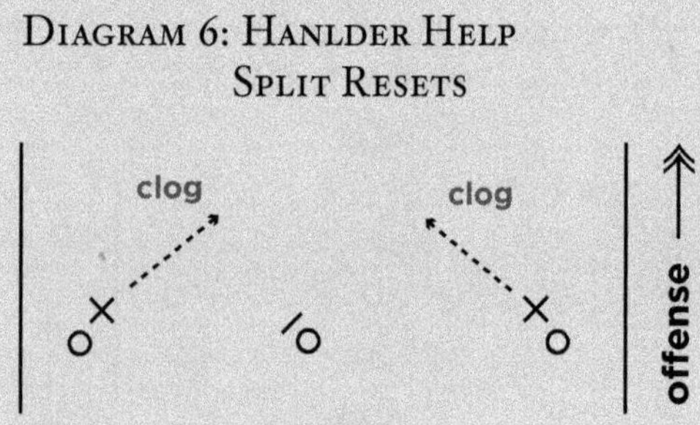

When the disc is splitting the two reset defenders, the classic help is to drop both defenders off into the cutting lanes and force the disc to the sideline. (Diagram 6) This is an excellent defense and I would highly recommend it against any team that is playing a traditional horizontal. The horizontal is very weak on the sideline; holding the offense pinned in this part of the field is what you want to do, so don't give up the free pass back to the middle.

You may have noticed major similarities between these moves and the cup work from a zone defense. This is a great observation and applying it will strengthen both your zone work and your help man techniques.

The last piece for this post is the concept of help in flow. Although this isn't technically handler help, it does involve helping from behind the disc. As play progresses down the field, there are many, many occasions where multiple offensive and defensive players are behind the disc. Typically, these defenders meekly trot along with their assignment, preparing for when it is their turn to play active defense again. Why?! Their assignment isn't doing anything and is in a horrible dead space position behind the disc! These defenders should put forth some effort, hustle downfield and into a throwing lane. They can clog up flow or slow a fast break, while simultaneously preparing for the moment when they'll have to recover back to their assignment. There is no current team that takes advantage of stay-on-your guy defending more than Revolver. Their cutters often delay their clears and repositions and lag behind the play for an extra second or two. This creates massive spaces downfield, but it also creates massive opportunities to help in flow.

~

A final note as I wrap up this series up for now. There is an assumption that help defense is soft or lazy; that somehow it isn't honest or doesn't express good Protestant work ethic values. A huge part of this comes from watching people who are soft or lazy playing poachy, soft and lazy defense so that the defense itself has taken on the persona of these practitioners. The best defenders in ultimate right now are the ones who can take the tough assignments without help. 'I can do it,' they think, 'so everyone else should be able to as well.' Help defense doesn't have to be lazily; done correctly it is actually far more work than vanilla defense is. If you use help in flow techniques, you'll be adding multiple 30 yard sprints to every point. The same is true of any flash and recover techniques. As for help defense being soft, it's all in how you play. Truly great defense will wed help concepts to tough, grinding, physical man-to-man.

61
HEALING THE BAD APPLE

On fixing that one problem

Published August 27, 2014

I've been doing a lot of thinking about leadership lately. I spoke at Melissa Witmer's coaching conference on the importance of teaching leadership and then immediately transitioned into actually teaching leadership as part of a new program at Seattle Youth Ultimate Camp. I've had a ton of great conversations with kids, with my co-teachers Alyssa Weatherford and Reid Koss and with guest speakers (Sarah Griffith, Ben Wiggins, Hannah Kawai and Spencer Wallace).

It's been one of those really wonderful experiences of getting so much information and ideas and exposure that it is impossible to process it all. I'll be going back over my notes and memories for weeks; I'll be sure to share the highlights.

One recurring theme was how to deal with the 'bad apple.' This issue came up in various forms as a question during my URCA talk and it's been one of the more pressing issues faced by the students in the leadership camp. How do you deal with a player who is causing problems on the team and resistant to changing their behavior? How do you deal with a captain who is out of sync with the rest of the team? I thought I did a pretty bad job answering these questions during the conference Q&A. Part of that is just not having enough data; each case is so individual. And yet, there are some real commonalities that run through all of these situations. Here is the answer I should have given:

PREVENTION IS THE BEST MEDICINE. A healthy team with a strong and positive team culture is very unlikely to have bad apple trouble. First, there are fewer unhappy players. It is a powerful feeling when a team is all driving in the same direction. The feeling of unity and direction makes everyone happier, so you are less likely to have a player become unhappy in the first place. Still, there are always people who are disappointed with their playing time or disagree about strategy or are just plain difficult. A healthy team culture inoculates the other players against the damage the bad apple can inflict. Basically, the players just don't care that much because the tone of the team is set by the team. This is where the Clown Tent can be a life-saver. The bad behavior becomes just another idiosyncrasy like tardiness or the drops. The team accepts it as a part of the person just as they accept that person's strengths. So, if you are having bad apple trouble, look first at your team culture and team systems. Are they in tip-top shape? If not, address both team and individual issues simultaneously or you will find yourself dealing with a similar problem in the very near future.

USE THE ONE-ON-ONE CONVERSATION OUTSIDE OF PRACTICE. This is the best single tool you have as a leader. By making the conversation private, you remove any difficulty that might come from loss of face. It is much easier to admit fault privately, where there is less loss of pride. By moving the conversation outside of practice, you move it away from the emotion of the moment. This allows for a more rational and unemotional conversation, and you'll need all the help you can get. Finally, go slowly and don't be afraid to take breaks. Talking about really difficult issues is difficult; it's okay to stop for a moment, breathe and collect your thoughts. Many people have excellent defense mechanisms that allow them to avoid truly facing issues; pausing will give you an opportunity to find your way through the maze. These conversations are tricky, difficult and emotional so give them the care they deserve.

THE BAD APPLE IS A LEADER. This is a person who has the emotional strength to be a giant pain in the ass. That's a person who is a leader. You want this person on your side.

BE HUMBLE. Put the team first. If you set out to win an argument, you've already lost. Even seeing it as an argument is setting yourself up to lose. The only thing that will truly convince this person that you are on the same page is to you put yourself behind the team.

CONSIDER THE NUCLEAR OPTION. Carefully. There are times and places where a player, captain or coach is so toxic and so unwilling to adjust their behavior that the only choice is to eject them from the team. Before you get here, I really encourage you to make sure you've exhausted all your other options because this is going to be a big mess for everyone involved and there is a non-zero chance that it will destroy your team. I was part of a team that chose the nuclear option and it was followed by a five year nuclear winter. Still, in the broader ultimate landscape there are a couple of teams a year that evict players or leaders, and it's usually for the better.

62
MICRO-POSSE

On small planning groups

Published September 3, 2014

One of the main curriculum points from the Seattle leadership camp was providing peer-to-peer feedback. I'd originally imagined this to include the introduction of some prompts and techniques for providing feedback in a positive way. We did cover these items, but as things fell out, we ended up spending a lot more time focusing on what we called a Micro-Posse. (More on the name later.) The essence of a Micro-Posse is a group of three to six teammates who are designated to provide feedback to each other. We were exposed to these ideas through Alyssa Weatherford and Reid Koss who shared the small group techniques that both Riot and Sockeye* use and immediately it made sense to employ that structure for the rest of camp. We used our Micro-Posses to provide peer-to-peer feedback and provide a venue for small group discussion.

Sockeye's small groups, called Hate Posses, focus on goal setting, analysis and feedback. Sockeye will often provide space for Posse meetings by cooling down together. That time can be used for something as simple as a check-in or could be more targeted, looking specifically at a team or individual goal. It also came up in the course of Riot's work that creating in-practice time to meet was essential. Everyone is present and committed at practice; expecting these kinds of groups to operate outside of practice is facilitating failure.

Riot's groups, called Micro Communities, function in a similar way and with similar goals. Given the name, it's not surprising that Riot does community building work with their Micro Community, often having internal competitions that pit the communities against each other. But the coolest thing I heard about is called hot-seat feedback. The person on the hot seat can open with a self assessment and then the rest of the group takes over. Taking turns, each member of the Micro Community delivers a positive and a delta. The person in the hot seat is forbidden to reply or question until the entire group has gone. At the end of the weekend, Reid, Alyssa and I did hot seat feedback about the week of camp. I'd been puzzling all week over something I called mecro, which is the implementation piece between the macro (big picture stuff) and the micro (the details). I'm generally a macro guy, but I'm also pretty good once things get down to the nitty-gritty; it's the in between stuff, the mecro, that causes me so much trouble. Both Reid and Alyssa had the same delta for me – that I've got to communicate better – and I had a little aha! Communicating the big picture I've built in my head will help bridge the gap for other people.

Better communicating could help cure my mecro woes. Would I have figured this out on my own? Probably not.

The language around these groups is really important in shaping people's expectations and experience. The campers had an immediate negative reaction to the name Hate Posse that took me by surprise. I had recognized 'Hate' as a classic example of Sockeye's joking, cavalier exterior. In a brilliant twist, the name makes the groups lighter (the name is a joke) and heavier at the same time (you're prepared for hard words). Riot's choice of Micro Community also communicates a message to the team about the essential nature of the group – community conveys trust and unity above all. Even something as subtle as 'delta' makes a difference. I usually cringe when I hear a 'good' comment paired with 'something you could do better', but as a math nerd, I liked the idea of a delta with its implication of change.

Returning to Seattle leadership camp, we decided we wanted to form small groups to use for the remainder of the weekend and we needed a name: Micro-Posse was the obvious choice. (Hate-Community was a distant second.)

63
WIN THE FIELDS

On goodbyes

Published October 22, 2014

I just came back to say goodbye.

Over the years that I've written Win the Fields, I've come to grow surprisingly attached and loyal to you, the readers. The readers who take the time to post thoughtful, insightful comments; the readers who email me with their questions; the readers who find me out in the world and tell me they enjoy my writing; the readers I never hear from…

So when circumstances demand that I quit writing on a weekly basis, I felt obligated to come back one last time to explain myself and to say goodbye.

I began writing Win the Fields out of necessity. The words were in me and they were demanding to be let out, like thousands of hornets caught in a jar, buzzing incessantly and bouncing against the glass. I also felt that ultimate needed what I had to say. There were things happening in ultimate that were bad, bad, bad. Things that were pushing the sport in an unhappy direction. Things that were widely misunderstood. A lot of what was bad about the sport at that time wasn't what was actually happening (although we were in a pretty rough patch). Instead, it was how people were talking about what was happening. Cheat to Win (Without Cheating) was the first incarnation of this motivation, but it wasn't the last. Throughout my writing, I have strived to say what was missing from the conversation. Ironically, I've had less and less to say because more and more is being said. When I began, there was little to no media coverage of ultimate. Now, two areas I'd written in extensively– straight reportage and analysis– are widely covered by other people.

But really, this isn't an artistic decision. It's a time decision. My family is at a crucial turning point: My youngest child entered school this fall and my wife returned to paid work after years of managing our home and homestead. Like all changes, this is a mixed blessing. Our bank account will be happier, but we will be more stressed and more harried. My freedom to say, "I've got to write my post tonight, can you cook/feed the chickens/put the kids to bed?" is gone.

I teach school for a living and it is an often frustrating experience. My school is in a small Oregon town and like most small communities, we are struggling economically. I don't know what 'winning' in this situation would be or if my definition of 'winning' is even possible, but I do know that I haven't consistently put time into finding out. Writing, editing and tending the comments takes somewhere between 2-10 working hours per post and another several mental hours composing and considering. Ask your friends who are teachers: "Would an extra eight hours a week help you?" My family and professional pressures had me seriously wrestling with whether or not I could continue to coach Oregon. I've committed to the team, but I still don't know what that commitment will look like and the ways it will be constrained. As a part of this overall time pressure, I decided I needed to shed all my other ultimate-related commitments, of which Win the Fields is one.

I don't really know what's next. I have a very big, very ambitious piece in development, but I haven't even looked at it since school began. I hope to look at it this weekend. I had hoped to look at it last weekend, too. And the weekend before that one. But I have tests to grade, my wife had to go off to a faraway meeting so I'll have the kids, there's laundry to do and the dump run, there's cider to re-rack and forts to build…

…but I know those hornets are still buzzing, buzzing, buzzing.

Goodbye. Good luck. Play well. Learn much. Thank you.

www.ingramcontent.com/pod-product-compliance
Lightning Source LLC
Chambersburg PA
CBHW060014100426
42740CB00010B/1482
* 9 7 8 0 9 9 6 3 1 0 7 2 7 *